Divine Downloads

DAILY DEVOTIONS

BOB HERNDON

WESTBOW
PRESS®
A DIVISION OF THOMAS NELSON
& ZONDERVAN

WestBow Press books may be ordered through booksellers or by contacting:

WestBow Press
A Division of Thomas Nelson & Zondervan
1663 Liberty Drive
Bloomington, IN 47403
www.westbowpress.com
844-714-3454

ISBN: 979-8-3850-2972-3 (sc)
ISBN: 979-8-3850-2973-0 (e)

Library of Congress Control Number: 2024914725

Print information available on the last page.

WestBow Press rev. date: 8/7/2024

Contents

Foreword ix

Introduction xi

A Different World 1

Act Like Family 3

Afraid of Hell? You Betcha! 5

All Call-Return To Me 7

All That Matters 9

Be A Barnabas 10

Be Kind 11

Be The Light 12

Believe 13

Be Steadfast 15

Bread Alone 16

Bring 'Em Back 17

Build Up, Don't Tear Down 18

Bumper Sticker 20

Can't Get There From Here 21

Cast Off the Darkness, Put On the Light 23

Christ Follower 24

Continue 25

Deliver Us From Evil 27

Do Not Be Afraid 28

Do Not Be Overcome By Evil 29

I Dreamed That Jesus Came Back 30

Empty! 31

Fellowship 32

Fishers of Men 33

Fulfill Your Ministry 34

Glorify God With One Voice 36

God's "Perfect Will"? 37

Grasshopper or Overcomer? 38

Grow and Bear Fruit 39

Hananiah, Mishael, and Azariah 41

Happiness 43

Have You Met Him? 45

He Made Us, Not the Other Way Around 47

He Set Them In the Firmament...48

He Stops the Storm 50

He Who Now Restrains 51

Heavenly Minded 53

Hindrance Is Not Defeat, Just Winning God's Way 54

His Benefits...56

I Knew You 58

I Know 60

I Pity the Fool 61

I Shall Not Be Moved 63

"I" 64

In Everything Give Thanks 66

IN HIM...67

In the Cleft of the Rock 68

In The Morning 69

Infinite 70

Insight...71

It Depends Upon How You Look At It.......................................72

Judgement Free Zone 74

Just Believe..75

Just Scratching the Surface..77

Last Night's Dream, Jesus Came Back 79

Leaven...80

Living In the Rock 82

Look Around You...84

It's Looking More Like What It Will Look Like 86

Love = Obey...88

If You Love Him, You Want To Keep His Commandments 90

Love Your Enemies 91

Love, Love, Love 93

New Creation 94

No Doubt 95

"Normal" Church 97

Not Troubled? 99

Nothing But Jesus 100

One Accord 102

One Church 104

One More Lap 106

Peace And Safety 107

Power In Numbers 108

Pride and Humility 110

Pride Goes Before Destruction 112

Problem Solved 114

Proclaim! 116

Ready When He Needs You 117

See That You Are Not Troubled 119

Sharing His Spirit-Always His Plan 120

Snake Dream 122

Soar 123

Something Impossible for God? 124

The Holy Spirit Will Guide You Into All Truth 125

Spirit to spirit 126

Still, Small, Voice 128

Striking Instead of Speaking 129

Talk To Him Like A Friend 131

Temples 132

That Great Light 133

The Daily Reset 135

The Divine Order 137

The Glory of His Presence 139

The Living Word 141

The Mess of Manasseh 142

The Peace of Jerusalem 144

The Reason Jesus Came 145

The Set Time 146

Things Above 147

Thirsty for God 148

This World Is Not My Home 149

Time to Live the Truth 151

True God is Creator 153

Two Choices 154

Vapor 155

Vines 156

Walk Close To Him 158

Until My Kingdom Comes 159

Wayfaring Stranger 161

We Are In That Time 163

We Are Protected 165

Well Done 166

When I Fall, I Will Arise 167

When You Pray 168

Who Is Your King? 169

Why By Faith? 170

"Woke" 171

Work In Me 173

Worshiping In One Accord 174

Write It Down 176

You Be the New You 177

Your Body Needs You 178

The Same Body 179

Foreword

Welcome to a slightly different devotional experience! When I began to write these devotionals, I wasn't planning on writing a devotional book. I would be reading God's Word, or taking my daily, morning, prayer walk and it was as if the Holy Spirit would "download" an idea or scripture to write about. I would begin to write the idea down and it would seem to flow as I typed it. I would average two or three a week, sharing them on my personal Facebook page or my Living Water group on Facebook. I began to write them and save them in Word in a folder and called it "Bob's Blogs". People began to message me and comment on the posts how they were encouraged and blessed by these devotionals and blogs. I would be at the grocery store and other public places and people who I never expected said that they read them every time I came out with them. Then, the idea came to me to put them in the form of a devotional book.

I, by no means, claim that these are inerrant, prophetic, epiphanies, that are designed to guide someone's life, but, I also know that I couldn't have written them without some inspiration from the Holy Spirit. These messages are hopefully, words of encouragement, inspiration, hope, wisdom, courage, and love. What's different about them is the way in which I am going to challenge you to read them. Rather than having placed them in numeric or chronological order with a date beside them, I have them listed in alphabetical order. Some may have been written two or three years ago and some as recently as this week. I encourage you to, pray first, then flip through or open the book randomly and read the devotional where you "land". I will have a few under specific topics, but for the most part, they are an extremely wide range of subjects and examples. Where there is room on the page, feel free to write notes or how the message relates to you. You can leave a check mark if you don't have anything to write. That way, you will know that you have already read it.

As I believe these "downloads" were inspired by the Holy Spirit, I believe if you use the method I just described, you will find that the topic will seem more than "coincidental" as to how it applies to your present situation. Of course, if you want to read them in the traditional way, one right after the other, you are welcome to do that too. I hope this book becomes an experience, not just an inspiration, as I share it with you.

Introduction

A few years ago, I realized that if I was going to post something on Facebook, it needed to be worthwhile and not a projection of me. I saw it as a useful tool to get the Message out to a world that needs to turn to Jesus. There were a lot of clever and catchy things already out there and I didn't want to post something that I wished I hadn't later. So I started posting Scripture. I would pray and listen. Sometimes something would jump out at me during my quiet time. I would pray and hope that it would be just the right words for someone that day. Even if I didn't hear anything specifically, it was God's Word and it wouldn't return void; it would help someone.

For the last one to two years, I had been doing that same thing and a topic or idea would come to me and I would begin to write. It was one of those things that I had to sit down and do right away or I would lose it. I learned that if I woke up at night with one of those thoughts and went back to sleep, I would wake up in the morning and it would be completely gone. I couldn't pull it up not matter how hard I tried. So I learned to keep a notepad by my bed and write down the verse or title. I would begin to type the next morning and the Holy Spirit would give me fresh thoughts and Scriptures to go along with it. Then, I would share it, hopefully to help someone who might need it that day. I hope, as you read these devotions, they will minister to you in the same way.

A Different World

Romans 8:6 (ESV) "For to set the mind on the flesh is death, but to set the mind on the Spirit is life and peace. [7] For the mind that is set on the flesh is hostile to God, for it does not submit to God's law; indeed, it cannot. [8] Those who are in the flesh cannot please God.

[9] You, however, are not in the flesh but in the Spirit, if in fact the Spirit of God dwells in you. Anyone who does not have the Spirit of Christ does not belong to him. [10] But if Christ is in you, although the body is dead because of sin, the Spirit is life because of righteousness. [11] If the Spirit of him who raised Jesus from the dead dwells in you, he who raised Christ Jesus from the dead will also give life to your mortal bodies through his Spirit who dwells in you."

When I was born again in 1971, I literally stepped into another world. I felt it, I knew it inside, but I had just entered in through the door with my eyes wide open and had no idea what was next. What had happened was, my old self died at that moment. My sins erased. Guilt gone. The darkness fled because I stepped into the Light and it came into me. My spirit was reborn and for the first time, I was alive! Yet it was just a taste of what it will be like when we step into Heaven itself when we leave this mortal body. Since then, I have had many other encounters, experiencing the kingdom of God in powerful and unforgettable ways, but one of the greatest realizations I have had is that His Kingdom is here right now and He wants us to recognize, encounter, and experience it every day. That's why 1 Thessalonians 5:17 says, "pray without ceasing". We have open access to the Kingdom of God 24/7. But it's not like, I have to stop what I'm doing and kneel down and pray. I have open, constant communication with the Holy Spirit available constantly because He lives inside of me now.

Jesus wants us to walk as closely to Him as possible all the time. That's what Romans 8 is talking about. Our part of this relationship is to keep our mind on Him. **Galatians 5:16** says, " But I say, walk by the Spirit, and you will not gratify the desires of the flesh." **Colossians 3:1-2** says, "If then you have been raised with Christ, seek the things that are above, where Christ is, seated at the right hand of God. Set your minds on things that are above, not on things that are on earth." God created mankind to walk and fellowship with Him. The more we do that, the more we do that. (What does that mean?) The more we walk closely to Jesus, the more we grow in our faith, we actually experience and see the Kingdom of God more clearly. We understand it more. Our lives change; our ambitions, our desires, our habits, and the amount of fruit that we bear. Just yesterday, I was looking back at myself only a few months ago and realizing how different I was then than I am now. That is what happens when we walk in the Spirit and live in the realm of the Kingdom. There are Christians who aren't much different now than the day they met Jesus. Has your life changed? If not, go back to that starting place you had with Jesus. This time, let Him take everything. Let go of "me" and "I", and let Him be Lord of everything in your life. Talk to Him regularly. Read His word every day. Start looking up and take your eyes off of this fallen world. In **Matthew 6:33,** Jesus said, "seek first the Kingdom of God and His righteousness, and all these things will be given to you."

Act Like Family

Psalms 133:1(NKJV) "Behold, how good and how pleasant *it is* for brethren to dwell together in unity!"

I was honored to sing at a friend's church last weekend with a group of singers who all came from different churches. We had Non-denominational, Baptist, Church of God of Prophecy, Methodist, and a few more I wasn't sure of. Some of these churches were small, some were large, some were old fashioned with almost no technology and others were loaded with the latest hi-tech. Some had a song leader, others had a worship team or a choir. As far as the music went that night, I sang one that was contemporary in around the 1600s, and one from the 70s and one that was only about 2 years old. We heard country, gospel, contemporary worship, original songs, and other styles. That night, we all were one body; we all fellowshipped and loved. Two of the ladies there were sisters whom I have known since they were kids. We used to go on retreats together and we talked about how this atmosphere seemed like one of those retreats. I said that it makes me think about what Heaven will be like, except Heaven will be that retreat that never ends. There will be love and fellowship and the presence of the Lord will not only be felt, but He will be there in the midst of us!

So…. we have a choice to make. Are we going to draw near to God and to each other? When we compete, complain, accuse, find fault, compare, cause division, throw out innuendos, sarcasm; none of that comes from God. In fact, God doesn't like it at all. Here's what He said about that: 1 **Corinthians 1:10 (ESV)** "I appeal to you, brothers, by the name of our Lord Jesus Christ, that all of you agree, and that there be no divisions among you, but that you be united in the same mind and the same judgment." **Isaiah 54:15 (ESV)** If anyone stirs up strife, it is not from me; whoever stirs up strife with you shall fall because of you.

There are tons of Scriptures about it, but this one kind of sums it up: "And be kind to one another, tenderhearted, forgiving one another, even as God in Christ forgave you.." (**Ephesians 4:32 NKJV**).

If you use Facebook, X, Instagram, personal conversations, pulpits, to run other believers down, you are completely out of God's will. The airwaves are full of programs, podcasts, interviews, and sermons that are devoted to tearing other believers down. They consist of individuals who feel that they are "called" to expose any mistakes or wrongdoing from virtually any other ministry who doesn't do it the way that they do. I have yet to find this "ministry" in the Bible, listed among the gifts in places like **Romans 12**, **1 Corinthians 12-14**, **Ephesians 4**, **Acts**, or anywhere else.

1 Peter 3:8 (ESV) "Finally, all of you, have unity of mind, sympathy, brotherly love, a tender heart, and a humble mind." The key is in the term, "humble mind". A humble mind is where it begins. A humble mind forgets about, "what's in it for me?", "my feelings were hurt", "I should be in charge", "that offends me", "that's not my agenda"… Now, let's back up to the first part of the verse. "Finally" (last, but certainly not least), "ALL of you have unity of mind" means that we have to purposefully decide to be one with each other. It is not our natural tendency. Then we should have "sympathy". We should care about how the other one feels and make that even more important than how we feel. Then it says, "brotherly love". We need to see each other as family even if the other one is completely different from us. Next it says to have a "tender heart". We need to be sensitive, not for ourselves, but for the other one. Jesus said to love the Lord with all our hearts, minds, souls, body and strength, then to love our neighbor as ourselves. I call that the "divine order". 1.God. 2.Others. 3.Self. That's the opposite of the world or natural order.

If we are all in one accord, we can expect things to happen like they did at the day of Pentecost in **Acts 2**. The Holy Spirit will pour out and accomplish His will. Miracles of all kinds and salvations will occur. We are living in a time when that is vital. The world is watching us. Let's not be their excuse to say they don't want to come to Jesus. Don't wait for the other person to ask forgiveness. You ask first and make things right even if you don't think you are wrong. Someone once said, "Jesus didn't die for right people; He died for wrong people. Let's confess our faults to each other and be of one accord. **James 5:16 (ESV)**- " Therefore, confess your sins to one another and pray for one another, that you may be healed. The prayer of a righteous person has great power as it is working." Amen

Afraid of Hell? You Betcha!

Matthew 10:28 (NKJV) "And do not fear those who kill the body but cannot kill the soul. But rather fear Him who is able to destroy both soul and body in hell."

Recently, I was talking to someone who had been reprimanded for using fear of Hell as a means of bringing people to Christ. I have heard this many times before. Something like, "I don't think you should use the fear of Hell to try to convert people. You should persuade them with God's love". Well, that sounds noble and spiritual, but it is just full of holes and is really just a cop-out. It also sounds as if one just loved God so much, that He reached down His hand and saved them because they deserved it. A nice word for that is, "balderdash" or just nonsense. First of all, it is saying that Jesus did it the wrong way. Jesus warned us of Hell more than anyone else in the Bible. In the KJV, He mentioned it 17 times. Nine times in the book of Matthew, Luke and Mark each three times, and in Revelation, He mentions it once (although it is in Revelation four times). The Bible itself has the word Hell in it a total of 54 times. That's not counting terms like "torment" that is mentioned twenty times, "Lake of Fire", four times, and other terms that describe it.

Jesus told us how horrific Hell is in Luke 16. After the rich man was thrown in "torment", he begged for a drop of water to touch the tip of his tongue for relief. He also begged that God would send Lazarus to go and warn his brothers about how horrible that place was. He was told, "no", because the law and the prophets (Scripture) should be enough. This was not a parable or a story. Jesus told the name of the righteous man and the actual conversation. Then Jesus told us in **Matthew 10:28** and **Mark 9:43-48** that it is to be avoided at all costs, even if it meant losing an eye or a hand. Jesus was not kidding around! I have read of many accounts of people who have coded in the hospital and been resuscitated and saw, at least, a glimpse of Heaven. I have also read of some who got a glimpse of Hell. The fear, pain, agony, hopelessness, darkness, stench, and more were always beyond description. I believe a ten second vision of Hell would result in PTSD for years.

The real reason that people say you shouldn't talk about Hell is that they don't believe in it or they don't want to. They are therefore calling Jesus a liar. I get it. I don't want to think about

Hell and it would be easier not to think about it if I could form a theology that would cause me to not believe in it. But if there is a dangerous pit in the direction I am walking, putting on a blindfold won't protect me from the pit. Instead, it will pretty much guarantee that I will fall in it.

Now, here comes the "love" part. **John 3: 16** "For God so loved the world that He gave His only begotten Son, that whoever believes in Him should not perish but have everlasting life.

17 For God sent not his Son into the world to condemn the world; but that the world through him might be saved."

Jesus gave His own life to save us from Hell, because He loves us. Jesus did all the hard part and we just need to believe. The night I gave my life to Christ, the Holy Spirit had been working overtime on me, drawing me to Him. I wanted Jesus because of His great love for me, but I started searching after I realized that on my present path, I was going to go to Hell, directly to Hell, do not pass "Go", etc. I realized I was lost and began to seek God. So, it was a combination of experiencing the love of God, the fear of God, the desire to go to Heaven, and fear of going to Hell that was working together in tandem to bring me to the place of repentance at the foot of the Cross. I did, and now I know Him and love Him and will follow Him all the rest of my life.

All Call-Return To Me

Joel 2:12 (ESV) "Yet even now," declares the Lord, "return to me with all your heart, with fasting, with weeping, and with mourning; [13] and rend your hearts and not your garments." Return to the Lord your God, for he is gracious and merciful, slow to anger, and abounding in steadfast love; and he relents over disaster.

This verse is an "all call". It's saying to all who have wandered off, "return to me". It's saying, He's giving to those who have strayed away, one last chance. There are some pretty scary verses out there about wandering away so far that you deny Christ again. **Hebrews 6:4-6** says, "For it is impossible, in the case of those who have once been enlightened, who have tasted the heavenly gift, and have shared in the Holy Spirit, [5] and have tasted the goodness of the word of God and the powers of the age to come, [6] and then have fallen away, to restore them again to repentance, since they are crucifying once again the Son of God to their own harm and holding him up to contempt." I have heard several explanations as to how those verses didn't really mean what they said, but I believe that it's pretty plain. Another scary verse is in **2 Peter 2:20** which says, "[20] For if, after they have escaped the defilements of the world through the knowledge of our Lord and Savior Jesus Christ, they are again entangled in them and overcome, the last state has become worse for them than the first. [21] For it would have been better for them never to have known the way of righteousness than after knowing it to turn back from the holy commandment delivered to them."

Some say that these people never really knew Jesus in the first place. Others say that they knew Him and turned away. Either way, the outcome is the same, but the actual verses sound like they really knew Him. I have been a Christian for 53 years now. Over that amount of time, I know people whom I have walked with, fellowshipped with, shared life with, who had a genuine, fruit-bearing, life with Christ, but later left Him. Some quit believing the Word and started believing something completely contrary, others went back into the old sins (and new ones) that held them captive, others go as far as openly denying Jesus and the Bible and trying to convince others to do the same. I know people who I would see crying and seeking God at the altar rail in church on a regular basis and now they are claiming to be agnostic or an atheist. In each case, something traumatic happened in their life, some major disappointment or tragedy took place, or they were deceived by someone who subtly influenced them. I remember a number of young people who were going into the ministry who I warned about the false teachers in "cemetery" (seminary). They chuckled and said not to worry. Some of them got caught up in the deception and swallowed the bait, hook, line, and sinker. They are now diligently deceiving others and denying God's Word.

Last night and this morning, I was led by the Holy Spirit to send out a message to these people. "RETURN TO ME"! The time is short and the rapture is coming. Those who have turned away will be left behind, but God is saying "return to Me" while this door is still open. He is knocking (**Rev. 3:20**). Repent and return to your first love (**Rev. 2:4-5**) and return back to that simple child-like faith (Matt. **11:25** and **19:14**). God will pick up where you left off just like the father with the prodigal son. He will restore all the time that was wasted (Joel 2:25) and He will still say, "well done" (**Matt. 25:21**) if you return now. So, "yet even now… return with all your heart". Thus says the Lord…Amen.

All That Matters

---

1 Corinthians 3:11 (ESV) "For no other foundation can anyone lay than that which is laid, which is Jesus Christ. 12 Now if anyone builds on this foundation with gold, silver, precious stones, wood, hay, straw, 13 each one's work will become clear; for the Day will declare it, because it will be revealed by fire; and the fire will test each one's work, of what sort it is. 14 If anyone's work which he has built on it endures, he will receive a reward. 15 If anyone's work is burned, he will suffer loss; but he himself will be saved, yet so as through fire."

I have a lot of wasted time in my day. I don't think that I will ever have a day where that doesn't happen. I can, however, make a conscious decision to utilize that time where I am building on the Foundation that Jesus gave me. It might be one thing today and something completely different tomorrow. The important thing is, we need to respond to how the Holy Spirit is moving in us as a vessel that day. Those things that we let the Holy Spirit do through us are the gold, silver, and precious stones on our Foundation. The things we do, whether selfish, sinful, or even good and noble, that we do out of our own motives and strength are the wood, hay, and stubble that will be tossed in the fire. Here's the difference: we do not need to work for God; we need to let God work through us. **Hebrews 11:6** says, "But without faith it is impossible to please Him…" **Romans 14:23** says, "for whatever is not from faith is sin." So how do you do that? **Proverbs 3:6** says, "In all your ways acknowledge Him, And He shall direct your paths." Acknowledge the Lord in what you do, commit your life, your day, your actions, your words to Him. All that matters is what He does in us and through us. Don't get discouraged when you fail to do that. Just do it again every time you get a chance. He wants you to keep on drawing near to Him because He loves you.

Be A Barnabas

Acts 4:36 (NKJV) "And Joses, who was also named Barnabas by the apostles (which is translated Son of Encouragement), a Levite of the country of Cyprus, [37] having land, sold *it,* and brought the money and laid *it* at the apostles' feet."

In these perilous times that we live in, we need encouragement. When we are down, we need someone to help us get up, not to tell us why we fell down. God does that with His grace. He already knows we messed up and loves us enough to forgive us and pick us up, dust us off, bandage the knee, and pat us on the bottom and say "keep on walking". Barnabas' real name was Joses. Barnabas was a nickname that meant, "son of encouragement". Encouragement really means to enable courage in someone. To help them to keep on walking. Let's let it be our goal to encourage everyone we are around today, especially those who are the hardest to encourage. They are the ones who need it most. It really will change things. Be a Barnabas.

Be Kind

Ephesians 4:32 (NKJV)
"Be kind to one another, tenderhearted, forgiving one another, as God in Christ forgave you."

You ever notice how it is easier, not to be kind to one who is closer to you? I'm talking about a spouse, sibling, parent or child, then the farther out the relationship is, the more we put forth effort to be kind. One reason is (the main one, I believe) that we expect our love relationship to be deeper, and thicker skinned, and we let down our guard. We "vent" upon each other. Logically you would think, the more you love, the kinder you would naturally be. There's the catch. We are not naturally kind. We have to put forth conscious effort. We have to choose to be kind every time we do it. Kindness does not come from the old fallen nature. It is a fruit of the Holy Spirit mentioned in Galatians 5. We can change the world with kindness. We can encourage someone, even make their day with it. Find the person or persons who you are not usually as kind to today and ask the Holy Spirit to manifest that fruit through you. Just remember, there are some of whom it won't come naturally, but we get it "supernaturally". (You could start with buying someone a Kind Bar <insert segoe UI emoji J-65>).

Be The Light

Ephesians 5:8 (ESV) "...for at one time you were darkness, but now you are light in the Lord. Walk as children of light [9] (for the fruit of light is found in all that is good and right and true), [10] and try to discern what is pleasing to the Lord. [11] Take no part in the unfruitful works of darkness, but instead expose them. [12] For it is shameful even to speak of the things that they do in secret. [13] But when anything is exposed by the light, it becomes visible, [14] for anything that becomes visible is light. Therefore it says,

"Awake, O sleeper,
and arise from the dead,
and Christ will shine on you."

[15] Look carefully then how you walk, not as unwise but as wise, [16] making the best use of the time, because the days are evil."

We, once, were not only walking in darkness; we were darkness. But now, since we have met Jesus Christ, WE ARE LIGHT in the Lord. We were once outside of the Lord, now, we are IN THE LORD (**2 Cor. 5:17**). Saints, there is nothing back there that is worth looking at. (**Luke 9:62** But Jesus said to him, "No one, having put his hand to the plow, and looking back, is fit for the kingdom of God.") Remember Lot's wife.

Let's be the light, let it shine, walk in it, and share it. Keep focused on that brilliant Light (Jesus, the Bright and Morning Star) until we are in our glorified bodies and can look directly at it. Then,

"Let your light so shine before men, that they may see your good works and glorify your Father in heaven." **Matthew 5:16**.

Believe

John 6:29 (NKJV) "Jesus answered and said to them, "This is the work of God, that you **believe** in Him whom He sent.""

John 6:35 "And Jesus said to them, "I am the bread of life. He who comes to Me shall never hunger, and he who **believes** in Me shall never thirst.""

Acts 16:31 "So they said, "**Believe** on the Lord Jesus Christ, and you will be **saved**, you and your household.""

Romans 10:9 "…that if you confess with your mouth the Lord Jesus and **believe** in your heart that God has raised Him from the dead, you will be saved."

Galatians 3:22 "But the Scripture has confined all under sin, that the promise by faith in Jesus Christ might be given to those who **believe**."

1 John 5:5 "Who is he who overcomes the world, but he who **believes** that Jesus is the Son of God?"

Genesis 15:6 "And he **believed** in the Lord, and He accounted it to him for righteousness."

John 1:12 "But as many as received Him, to them He gave the right to become children of God, to those who **believe** in His name:"

John 3:15 "…that whoever **believes** in Him should not perish but have eternal life."

John 3:16 "For God so loved the world that He gave His only begotten Son, that whoever **believes** in Him should not perish but have everlasting life."

The word **"believe"** is written 270 times in the New King James Version. In most cases, it is talking about having access to God and His kingdom in some way. It is the only word that stands alone without needing help from any other word to have eternal life. Just ask the thief on the cross. In **Genesis 3:1-5**, Satan tempted Adam and Eve to not **believe** God's word and they yielded. That moment is where the fall began. Everything that is wrong in the world is wrong because of that moment. Satan is still trying his best to keep people away from believing. From the human traffickers to theologians, if he can convince people not to believe God's Word, he will keep the world in the shape it is in. **Jesus** came and did what no one else could do. He became our last Adam (**1 Cor. 15:45**) and made things right again, but there is only one way to get back on that right side. **Believe.** Re-read all the scriptures above. Move from the original unbelief where Adam and Eve, who had dominion over all the world with God, handed it over to Satan. Now God hands it back over to us if we will just… **believe.**

Be Steadfast

"Blessed is the man who remains steadfast under trial, for when he has stood the test he will receive the crown of life" **James 1:12 (ESV)**

Jesus' ultimate trial in the last days before the death on the cross and resurrection began in the olive press of prayer in Gethsemane. At that point, He even asked the Father if there was any other way, to take this cup from Him. He ended with, "nevertheless not My will, but Yours, be done." (Luke 22:42). Jesus, operating in His state of being "fully man" at that moment, completely laid down His life, His comfort, everything on this earth to fulfill the will of the Father. He received the crown of life and gives each one of us a crown of life. He was steadfast so that we can be steadfast. What He did by Himself, we can do with Him inside of us. We simply rely on Christ in us (the hope of Glory, **Col. 1:17**) and we will be able to do it because He has already done it and will continue to do it through us. (**Philippians 4:13** "I can do all things through Christ who strengthens me.")

Bread Alone

Matthew 4:4(NKJV) "But He answered and said, "It is written, 'Man shall not live by bread alone, but by every word that proceeds from the mouth of God.' "

In the book of Revelation, the last two chapters are talking about the New Heaven and Earth. While praying this morning and watching the birds, I was thinking about how the very basic, primary function of a human (and pretty much, every living thing) is to eat to stay alive. Then, I thought about Heaven and the primary function of every being different. It is to worship the Creator and fellowship with and love Him and each other. Yes, it does say that there is fruit, a wedding feast, and other indicators of food that probably surpasses anything we've ever imagined here, but that won't be our primary function. We won't have to eat to survive, we will be filled with life from the Source of life.

Jesus already knew that. He knew that the source of eternal life was from God, supplied to us by His Word. **Romans 8** and **Galatians 5** tells us to walk in the Spirit, not the flesh. **Romans 6** and 7 and many other places tell us to put the flesh to death by being crucified with Christ so we can be resurrected by Him. In **Matthew 6:33**, Jesus said to seek first the kingdom of God and all these things (including bread) would be added to us. He was saying that we can start changing those priorities by entering into His presence and His kingdom now. Another way to put it is, we exchange the temporary bread for the Living Bread. **John 6:35** And Jesus said to them, "I am the bread of life. He who comes to Me shall never hunger, and he who believes in Me shall never thirst."

Bring 'Em Back

James 5:19 (ESV) "My brothers, if anyone among you wanders from the truth and someone brings him back, ²⁰ let him know that whoever brings back a sinner from his wandering will save his soul from death and will cover a multitude of sins."

God is calling His "prodigals" home. The harvest is ripe and He needs His laborers working for Him. Some are like sheep who have gone astray. When they wandered away from the Shepherd, they found themselves in a confused mess with no peace. Let's pray for them and invite them back to that place with Jesus, their first love, as if they never left. You'll be surprised how many will say, "yes". Who do you ask? Who is that person who has been on your mind lately? Pray first. Then ask. Watch what God will do!

Build Up, Don't Tear Down

Ephesians 4:29 (ESV) "Let no corrupting talk come out of your mouths, but only such as is good for building up, as fits the occasion, that it may give grace to those who hear."

Social media is just a thing. It can be used to bless or curse. It can be used to build up or to tear down. I see it as a tool, and usually not a source of entertainment, news, or gossip. There are a lot of comments that I want to chime in on, but I just pause and take a breath and say, "will this build up or tear down?" This verse in Ephesians says it all. It is talking to all Christians. Our job is to bless and not curse; to build up and not tear down. I am not in 100% agreement with any other believer in Christ out there. Some I am 99% with and others more like 40%, but if they are truly believers, they are truly children of God, my brothers and sisters, and I am commanded to do nothing but love them. I even find that I can learn things from them, sometimes I am even wrong. (Imagine that!)

I have seen people who use the label of Christian engage in tearing other Christians down. I have even seen Scripture used to get in a "dig" or try to tear down. I have seen Christians get involved in conspiracy theories that are contrary to God's Word. I have seen posts that agree with hateful comments and some of our dear church folk using profanity. Many times, they say they are "venting". The problem is, they are expressing thoughts that are out of control and letting the whole world hear them. I recently saw one that was falsely accusing a church and individuals, and people were chiming in and throwing in their opinions based upon something that was completely false. The most tragic part was, non-believers were using that as fuel to justify why they didn't go to church. I was talking to one of the people who was accused and this verse came to me:

Matthew 5:11 "Blessed are you when others revile you and persecute you and utter all kinds of evil against you falsely on my account. 12 Rejoice and be glad, for your reward is great in heaven, for so they persecuted the prophets who were before you." Also, Romans **12:14** says, "Bless those who persecute you; bless and do not curse them."

So, here we are. **James 3:10** says, " From the same mouth come blessing and cursing. My brothers, these things ought not to be so. The rest of the chapter in **Ephesians 4** says, " [30] And do not grieve the Holy Spirit of God, by whom you were sealed for the day of redemption. [31] Let all bitterness and wrath and anger and clamor and slander be put away from you, along with all malice. [32] Be kind to one another, tenderhearted, forgiving one another, as God in Christ forgave you.

1 John 4:7-8 says, "Beloved, let us love one another, for love is from God, and whoever loves has been born of God and knows God. 8 Anyone who does not love does not know God, because God is love."

Do you love Jesus? Love each other. Build each other up; don't tear down. If you are getting that urge or "feeling" to say something harmful about someone, it is not coming from the Holy Spirit; it is coming from that other one. Will it produce love, joy, peace, gentleness, kindness, goodness, self-control, patience, faith? That is the fruit of the Holy Spirit in **Galatians 5:22-23**. The rest of the chapter goes like this: "[24] And those who belong to Christ Jesus have crucified the flesh with its passions and desires. [25] If we live by the Spirit, let us also keep in step with the Spirit. [26] Let us not become conceited, provoking one another, envying one another."

Bumper Sticker

I saw a bumper sticker that said "Religion; because thinking is hard". I thought how utterly opposite of the truth this is. Thinking and logic would tell you that no matter if you wait 14 billion years or 14 quintillion years, nothing can produce nothing. If you take one day to study all of the things that take a perfect balance to even exist; whether it be an atom, any part of the human body, the ecosystem, the orbit of the earth or the "wobble" in its rotation that provides perfect synchrony, the position of the earth with the sun (if it were off by a few miles one way or another, we couldn't exist), or the billions of the rest of the examples I could use, we could not exist without a Creator. One mathematician/scientist figured, if there were 10 to the twentieth power planets in the universe just like earth (we only know of one) and they all had the "primordial soup" needed to accidentally create life with the sun rays, oxygen, etc., the chances of it happening would be 10 to the 415th power to one against it forming. (That's 10 with 415 zeroes behind it). In science, if something is 10 to the 50th power to one against it, it is considered scientifically impossible. So, without all those added features (the right ingredients, the sun, the oxygen, etc.) and only one planet, another scientist said that the chances are 10 to the (almost) 50,000th power to one against it. It looks to me like it takes a lot more faith to NOT believe in God than to believe. C.S. Lewis, one of the most intelligent men that we knew of, set out to disprove God and after a lot of honest attempts, finally conceded that there had to be a God. He became one of the staunchest defenders of the faith in the 20th century.

So, Religion? Maybe, but knowing the Creator, who gave His Son, Jesus Christ, to be Him, as one of us, is the most intelligent thing a person can do. Here's my theory on those who don't want to believe and try to evangelize it; 1. They have a beef with God about something that went wrong in their life, 2. They are living in a way that they know doesn't line up with God's will, or 3. (as in all cases) They have just been totally deceived by satan. Or, 4- **Psalms14:1 (NKJV)**

"The fool has said in his heart,
"There is no God."
They are corrupt,
They have done abominable works,
There is none who does good."

Can't Get There From Here

John 14:6(NKJV) "Jesus said to him, "I am the way, the truth, and the life. No one comes to the Father except through Me."

Matthew 7:13-14 "Enter by the narrow gate; for wide is the gate and broad is the way that leads to destruction, and there are many who go in by it. Because narrow is the gate and difficult is the way which leads to life, and there are few who find it."

Imagine if someone wanted you to come visit them at a place so wonderful that you can't even imagine it. Then they give you the directions on a map, they write down the places to turn and landmarks to watch for. Then, after all that, you put it on your GPS, program it to whatever voice, language, and accent you like, and you're on your way. But something happens on the way. You see a road that looks like a much better way to get there. It is much wider and smoother. The speed limit is higher. There are beautiful hills, trees, lakes and towns on the way. The written directions and maps do not tell you to go that way. The GPS says, "redirect", "make a u-turn", "take the next right", etc. You say, "no, this way looks right, I'm gonna do it my way." Well, at the end of the beautiful road, you find that it just abruptly ends and if you don't stop in time, you will run off the end which was not finished because they were waiting for the bridge over the canyon to be finished. If you are driving blindly, not paying attention, and have your eyes on other things, you will run off into the canyon.

I'll bet you've already figured out what I'm saying. God has invited us to come to His kingdom. The map and written directions are the Bible and the GPS is God's Paraclete Spirit (GPS). (**John 14:16**, Jesus called Him the Comforter, translated from Greek word, "Paraclete". It worked in "GPS"). So the directions are written and drawn in God's Word, but the Holy Spirit helps to interpret these directions so you will understand them. Jesus said, "I Am the Way." The directions in the Bible all point to Jesus. Jesus paid the tolls. He paved the roads. He made the crooked ways straight, the rough places smooth. He brought down the mountains and raised the valleys. He did it all for you. Now, He says to start driving and follow Him. In the book, *Pilgrim's Progress*, the pilgrim named Christian got off of the Heavenly Highway, following what looked like a much smoother road, and wound up in the castle of Giant Despair. There he was imprisoned, beaten, tortured, and almost starved. Later the King sent a way of escape and he, being bruised, bloody and hungry, got back on the King's road. Some of you may have been trying to get to God your own way. You may have already begun to suffer the consequences, but you haven't run off of the cliff yet. God is saying, "Get back on My highway and come home!"

Cast Off the Darkness, Put On the Light

Romans 13:12 (ESV)
"The night is far gone; the day is at hand. So then let us cast off the works of darkness and put on the armor of light."

In the month of the year when the days get noticeably shorter and it gets dark more quickly. The world even celebrates that darkness with all kinds of spookiness and scary stuff. Many take it lightly and others take it more seriously. Some take it back to the roots of Paganism and the Druids in ancient Celtic culture. Some involved in witchcraft and Satanism make Samhain (Halloween) their highest unholy day. There are different reactions among Christians to this; some take it lightly and try to have fun with it and others take it more seriously and avoid it completely. When I was a youth pastor, we would take the youth out and pass out tracts, witness, and "take back the night" (not that we ever lost it). Sometimes we would have worship events to do the same.

Here's my take on it now: Every day is either a day of darkness or a day of light. The world is so full of darkness that God's people need to be letting the light shine brightly as long as we are here. I don't mean just smiley faces and "have a blessed day", I mean to share the new life that Jesus has given us when He put His Spirit in us. After that first encounter with Christ, we need to continue to renew it every day, casting off the darkness and putting on the light, growing deeper in our relationship and letting the Light shine more. Jesus said in **Matthew 5:16**, "Let your light so shine before men, that they may see your good works and glorify your Father in heaven."

Christl Follower

Mark 8:34 (NKJV)

"When He had called the people to *Himself,* with His disciples also, He said to them, "Whoever desires to come after Me, let him deny himself, and take up his cross, and follow Me. ³⁵ For whoever desires to save his life will lose it, but whoever loses his life for My sake and the gospel's will save it. ³⁶ For what will it profit a man if he gains the whole world, and loses his own soul? ³⁷ Or what will a man give in exchange for his soul? ³⁸ For whoever is ashamed of Me and My words in this adulterous and sinful generation, of him the Son of Man also will be ashamed when He comes in the glory of His Father with the holy angels."

The word Christian means "Christ follower". Jesus didn't say "if anyone wants to try Me out and see if it fits you". He didn't tell us if it made us feel good, or if it was convenient, or if we understood it. Here is the One who is the Way back to the Father, who tells us how (the Truth) and gave His life for us so we can have Life (**John 14:6**). Imagine, you are out in the wilderness, surrounded by snakes, scorpions, wild animals, and the buzzards are circling waiting for a meal. You can't see any sign of civilization or even water. Someone drives up in their desert vehicle and says, "get in with me, I'll take you out of here to my home where everything is safe and wonderful." That Guy is Jesus. His vehicle is the cross. We escape the old life by crucifying it and receive our new life by believing on Jesus and trusting completely in Him, thus allowing Him to come in us and bring us to life by being born again (**John 3:3**). So, taking up His cross is not "trying Him out", it is letting the old you die so He can make you into a brand-new being. Then, you can follow Him and enter in to His kingdom.

Continue

2 Timothy 3:14 (ESV) "But as for you, continue in what you have learned and have firmly believed, knowing from whom you learned it ¹⁵ and how from childhood you have been acquainted with the sacred writings, which are able to make you wise for salvation through faith in Christ Jesus. ¹⁶ All Scripture is breathed out by God and profitable for teaching, for reproof, for correction, and for training in righteousness, ¹⁷ that the man of God may be complete, equipped for every good work."

I remember my first year in an Old Testament class at a Methodist College (which no longer exists) in 1973. On the first day of class, our professor told us to forget everything our parents and grandparents taught us and for us to discover our "own faith" in our "own way". We heard that from some other classes that same semester. To many young, green, 18 year olds, that sounded glorious and liberating. To those of us who knew Jesus and had the Holy Spirit living inside of us, alarm bells were going off all over the place. The first Scripture that came to mind was "Honor thy father and mother", and many more. Unfortunately, many of the young students did just that; they forgot, they formed their own beliefs, and they did not continue in the faith of their fathers.

Paul's first letter to Timothy told what the reprobate generation would look like in the end times (chapter 3). His second letter (also chpter 3) told how they would get there with this admonition to continue in what they had learned from the Scriptures since their childhood. All throughout Biblical and secular history, right and wrong would get diluted, polluted, and convoluted as time went on. It fits under the second law of thermodynamics called "entropy", where if something is not maintained, it degenerates. You don't maintain your house, it falls in. The same for your yard, your car, your body, your mind, and even your faith. Faith is the most important of them all because it affects your eternity, long after the houses, yards, and cars are gone.

How do I maintain my faith? First, you feed it the proper, healthy food which is the Word of God that comes from hearing it taught and preached, and maybe, more importantly, we read the Bible every day. There are a lot of good "supplements" and "side dishes" out there which are devotional books, teaching books, testimonials, etc. But the main staple which must be consumed every day is the Bible, and when we read it, we ask the Holy Spirit to turn that "light" on and help us to understand it. That involves prayer, which is another vital part of this holy maintenance. Our relationship with the Lord is kept and made stronger by prayer, which is just talking to Him throughout the day. Another vitally important part is fellowship. We need each other to encourage, help, correct, and love us. Finally, the part of maintaining our own physical bodies which requires us to say "no" to laziness, is exercise. Our spiritual exercise is going out and sharing what we took in from our prayer and Word time. We tell people what Jesus did for us. We usually do that by doing; by helping them, by giving to them, by loving them, and at the same time, telling them. When we do all these things, we not only "keep the faith", we grow stronger in it.

Deliver Us From Evil

Matthew 6:13 (NKJV) "And do not lead us into temptation, But deliver us from the evil one. For Yours is the kingdom and the power and the glory forever. Amen."

Usually, I use what we call "The Lord's Prayer" as an outline for my prayer time. I start out with worship and praise, ask for His kingdom to come, for Him to fill me with the Holy Spirit, so that His will can be done through me today. Then the daily bread consists of, what is the word of the day from Jesus to me? Then, we get into the spiritual warfare, leading us away from temptation and delivering us from the evil one. I think how many times God has protected us from the schemes of the devil. I would have been dead a long time ago if it weren't for God's protection, leading constantly, having angels intervene. Yes, we need to pray daily for Him to deliver us from the snares of the devil.

Ephesians 6:12 says, "For we do not wrestle against flesh and blood, but against principalities, against powers, against the rulers of the darkness of this age, against spiritual *hosts* of wickedness in the heavenly *places.* ¹³ Therefore take up the whole armor of God, that you may be able to withstand in the evil day, and having done all, to stand. And **2 Corinthians 10:4** says, "For the weapons of our warfare are not carnal but mighty in God for pulling down strongholds,".

I know that God has protected us so many times that we weren't aware, but He leaves us our part. Pray, stay in fellowship with Him, and draw as close to Him as we can.

James 4:7 Therefore submit to God. Resist the devil and he will flee from you. ⁸ Draw near to God and He will draw near to you. Cleanse *your* hands, *you* sinners; and purify *your* hearts, *you* double-minded.

Do Not Be Afraid

In **Luke 1:13 (NKJV)**, the angel said, "**Do not be afraid**, Zacharias, for your prayer is heard; and your wife Elizabeth will bear you a son, and you shall call his name John. In **Luke 1:30,** Gabriel said to Mary, "**Do not be afraid**, Mary, for you have found favor with God. In **Matthew 1:20,** it says, "behold, an angel of the Lord appeared to him in a dream, saying, "Joseph, son of David, **do not be afraid** to take to you Mary your wife, for that which is conceived in her is of the Holy Spirit." In **Luke 2:10,** "Then the angel said to them (the shepherds), "**Do not be afraid**, for behold, I bring you good tidings of great joy which will be to all people."

There were things to be afraid of. Zacharias could lose his credibility as a priest and head of a family, Mary could lose her good name, reputation, husband, and even her life. Joseph could, and probably would lose his good name, future, family, home. The shepherds, well, for all they knew, they were about to lose their lives, seeing angels in their glory and shining in their brightness. Then there was the unseen. Satan did not want this child to be born. He wanted to send every demon, soldier, king, and even unfriendly people like the innkeeper to thwart the coming of the Messiah. I think the warfare could be felt in the natural realm. I believe there was a tangible oppression that could be felt in the air and the moods and attitudes of the people. Have you ever felt like there were times that doing God's will was like trying to wade through a swamp, or even quicksand? That's usually a sign that there's spiritual resistance. We need to look back and remember the words, "**do not be afraid**". Trudging forward, or marching on, or running into the face of the enemy is an act of faith. Shrinking back and quitting is what the angels were admonishing these people not to do. I believe that the very presence of Gabriel and the angels was saying "**fear not, because we've got this**".

We are in a time where the words "**do not be afraid**" or "**fear not**" are of the utmost importance. We are the ones called to bring God's light, the Good News, to the world. We have the Light, Jesus Christ, living inside of us and we are to bring it to the dark and lost world. We have been given the orders, "**fear not**" and we can take the same words to this world. We have His angels, His Word, His Spirit, saying "**we've got this**". We need to be those messengers that say, "**do not be afraid**, the Messiah has come, and He wants to come inside of you."

Do Not Be Overcome By Evil

"Do not be overcome by evil, but overcome evil with good." **Romans 12:21 (NKJV)**

When you look at the last part of Romans 12, you see Paul repeating what Jesus said in the Sermon on the Mount in Matthew 5-7. Here's the rest of it:

"14 Bless those who persecute you; bless and do not curse. 15 Rejoice with those who rejoice, and weep with those who weep. 16 Be of the same mind toward one another; do not be haughty in mind, but associate with the lowly. Do not be wise in your own estimation. 17 Never repay evil for evil to anyone. Respect what is right in the sight of all people. 18 If possible, so far as it depends on you, be at peace with all people. 19 Never take your own revenge, beloved, but leave room for the wrath of God, for it is written: "Vengeance is Mine, I will repay," says the Lord. 20 "But if your enemy is hungry, feed him; if he is thirsty, give him a drink; for in so doing you will heap burning coals on his head."

Just yesterday, I was thinking about ways to confront someone who was doing something that was just plain wrong. I had planned out several frontal attacks and comments I could make that they would not be able to refute. I was texting a friend who was talking about the sermon at church that morning that talking about resting in the Lord while He prepares a table in the presence of His enemies (Psalms 23). He said he had been spending so much time fighting instead of resting. That threw cold water on my thoughts and plans. It brought me back in line with God's Word and will. A couple of my weakest areas where I respond immediately without taking time to think are when someone does something, like pulling out in front of me, when driving, and when I am falsely accused of something. I want to react immediately. This temptation is there in a host of other areas in my life also. My prayer is, "Lord, help me to learn to let You fight my battles and help me to rest in You". Also I want to pray for Him to help me go a step beyond and bless those who persecute me, take advantage of me, talk about me, spit in my face, and all the rest. Help me to heap the love of Jesus on each one. I have literally seen this change some of the people who do these things. Amen

I Dreamed That Jesus Came Back

Revelation 20:6 (NKJV)
"Blessed and holy is he who has part in the first resurrection. Over such the second death has no power, but they shall be priests of God and of Christ, and shall reign with Him a thousand years."

Last night, I dreamed that Jesus came back, in fact, this is still "last night" because I got up to write it before I forgot any of it. Miraculously, I am sitting here typing without my glasses, because I forgot them and I don't even want to get up and get them so I don't lose my train of thought. This is not a dream about the Rapture (I had one of those about 40+ years ago). This is about the literal Second Coming of Christ.

All I can tell you is, we were in our immortal bodies. We couldn't be killed, and we had nothing to fear, ever, again. Jesus had just gotten here and was taking charge in His rule of the earth. In this dream, I remember being able to communicate with people who were hundreds of miles away without a phone or anything electronic. We would just set our minds on the Heavenly realm and it was like we would rise up above where we were, even our time we were in, and communicate. We were the Saints, who were already working with Jesus and we were establishing everything and putting everything and everyone in order under Jesus' reign. The wonderful thing was, just as you would imagine, Jesus was right there in the mix of things, walking around with His people. He wasn't in some distant office or on a throne far away. He was walking right there among us. Even though He was in the midst of it all, when I walked by Him, He looked at me and smiled and came up and hugged me, as I did Him, and we held each other, and I wept. Right then, I was included in the work that was being done and I was a part of it all. Then I woke up.

Empty!

Luke 24:6 (NKJV) "He is not here, but is risen! Remember how He spoke to you when He was still in Galilee."

There are two sites in Jerusalem that are potentially the tomb of Jesus. One has a massive, ornate, system of church buildings built over it. The Armenians, Greek Orthodox, and Roman Catholics all have their own wing covering it. There, they have a stone that was supposed to have been used for the preparation of Jesus' body for burial. Many believe that actually was the site where Jesus lay for 3 days. The tomb was hidden beneath all the ornateness, so no one could see it.

Then, there is the site of the Garden tomb. There is a society of women from Great Britain who have been keeping this site looking beautiful for over a century. One very adept and charming Irish lady explained that the rock we were looking at was Golgotha (the hill of the skull, which looked like a skull). The crosses where the crucifixions took place were right beside the road where people could look directly at them, taunt, curse, spit, and jeer at them.

Just a few yards further down the wall was a tomb that was carved out by hand. We were allowed to go into the first part of it and see the slab, table, and other things that would be needed. Before we went in, I saw some young, college aged ladies with a wide smile on their faces, saying, "affirmed"! "It's empty"! I went in next and looked at the simple, empty tomb. Sure enough, it was empty! I know we believers already know that, but there was just something about seeing it that made me want to break down. It made me want to give thanks for the greatest action that ever took place in the universe, the resurrection of the Man who is God, and God who became man and never sinned. The only one who did not deserve to die, gave His life so that everyone who would receive Him could have eternal life. And it happened in that simple, little tomb.

Fellowship

Acts 2:42 (NKJV) "And they continued steadfastly in the apostles' doctrine and fellowship, in the breaking of bread, and in prayers."

Fellowship. One person said it was two or more fellows on one "ship". If you think of the rough sea being the world with all the sin and darkness, we don't want to be out there trying to stay afloat by treading water. We need each other. Let's take advantage of it while we can. In many parts of the world, people are risking their lives every time they go to church, yet they keep going because they see the necessity and value of it. Find a good, solid, Bible preaching, God worshipping, Holy Spirit moving Gospel ship to worship in.

Fishers of Men

Matthew 4:19 (NKJV)
"Then He said to them, "Follow Me, and I will make you fishers of men.""

When I was a kid, one of the things I would get the most excited about would be when my dad would say that we were going fishing the next morning. Sometimes, we would get up as early as 4:00 a.m. to get out on the water by daybreak, when the crappie and bass were feeding. Other times, we would camp out and run our trotlines several times and bring home a "mess" of catfish, etc. As a result, when I grew up, fishing was one of my favorite activities in life, to the point of me buying a number of different kinds of fishing boats and gear. As a Christian, I would find that it was a combination of worldly pleasure and a time to be alone with God out in nature. Literally, "the best of both worlds".

Now, as I am older, I certainly have no qualms about fishing, but I find that I have a lot more joy and lasting pleasure from leading a person to Christ. Sometimes Jesus still takes me out to the water, just to be alone with Him, but most of the time, He leads me to the "sea" of humanity where there are still a lot of "fish" to be caught. When we share our testimony with someone, we are casting out line to invite them into the Kingdom of God. In the last few years, I have seen a surprising willingness of people to receive the Good News. Sometimes, I would be shocked that they were so eager to say "yes" and pray with me right there on the spot. In my own driveway, I have been privileged to pray with two delivery men from two different companies, to accept Jesus as their Lord and Savior. I got to pray with one person in the grocery store parking lot to be saved after just asking him if he knew Jesus. He said, "no". I said, "do you want to now?" He said, "yes". And we prayed. He is still walking with Jesus and attending church.

I am saying this to tell you, the fish are biting. They are hungry. Jesus is calling us to go fishing. Let's' go! You say, what kind of bait do I use? Just be you, with Christ inside of you, full of the Holy Spirit. He will do the rest.

Fulfill Your Ministry

Colossians 4:17 (NKJV) "… take heed to the ministry which you have received in the Lord, that you may fulfill it."

As I was reading God's Word this morning, I asked if there was any particular Scripture for me today. Immediately, Colossians 4:17 came to mind. Of course, the first thing I did was to question whether that was the Holy Spirit or just me. I didn't even remember if Colossians 4 had seventeen verses. When I turned to it, it began with "Say to Archippus…" Then the rest of the verse was like the Batman signal shining in the sky. "Take heed…" make sure, make it a priority, make sure you do it. The English Standard Version says ""See that you fulfill the ministry that you have received in the Lord." This has a sound of finality in it. It reminds me when I was a character coach for our local football team and the fourth quarter would get here. We would hold up four fingers reminding each other that this was the time to take care of business; to close it out. Time for the defense to dig in and for the offence to make that score. After this quarter, it would be win or lose.

That is the sense I felt this morning when I read this. While walking outside and praying, I thought back to when I was first born-again. I remembered the different chapters of my life and realized that they were all part of the ministry God had given me. Some seemed successful, others seemed like total flops and yet other times seemed not-so-significant. Then, I came back to the present and thought, all of these times were significant in one way or another to bring me to this time now. It's the fourth quarter, the last chapter, time to focus on the end of the game. Does this sound morbid or like I am preparing to die? No, this sounds like it should have all along. The team that plays with fourth quarter intensity the whole game wins. God is calling all His people to hold up the four fingers. If you are a believer in Jesus Christ, you have a ministry. **2 Corinthians 5:18** says, "All this is from God, who through Christ reconciled us to himself and gave us the ministry of reconciliation." Once you are saved, your job is to bring others to Christ. We are living in a time when we are called to step up, go out, and shine.

Billy Graham said "Many people are willing to have Jesus as part of their lives—as long as it doesn't cost them anything. They may even profess faith in Jesus and join a church. But

Jesus to them is almost like an insurance policy—something they obtain and then forget about until they die. But Jesus calls us to follow him every day." God is calling His people to do just that. Follow Him every day. Go to your job, your school, the marketplace, whatever you do and follow Jesus. Refocus on what you are here for. Ask, "How can I do your will today?" Bring someone to Jesus. Fulfill your ministry.

Glorify God With One Voice

Romans 15:5-6 (ESV) "May the God of endurance and encouragement grant you to live in such harmony with one another, in accord with Christ Jesus, 6 that together you may with one voice glorify the God and Father of our Lord Jesus Christ."

In **Genesis 11:4-8**, when the people of Shinar decided to build themselves a tower to the heavens, they were in one accord. God said, "Behold, the people is one, and they have all one language; and this they begin to do: and now nothing will be restrained from them, which they have imagined to do." We know the rest of the story where God came down, scattered them and confused their language.

God saw that they had evil intentions, yet they would have fulfilled them if He had not intervened because they were unified. Just think how much more can be accomplished if we are like-minded for the right reason with the power of the Holy Spirit in us! The first thing that comes to mind is **Acts 2** when they were all seeking God in one accord and the Holy Spirit fell. That was a dividing point in history that made it possible for us to all have that personal relationship with God and His power to live it.

In **John 14**, Jesus said that we would do greater things than even He did, because He was going to go to the Father. The only way that would be possible is if He continues to live on the earth through us. That is the result of the day of Pentecost. That is the result of people seeking God in one accord. What will happen if we continue to seek God together, believing in His Word in faith? We won't be building the Tower of Babel (self-centered), we will be building the Kingdom of God while we are on this earth (focused upon God).

The devil is deceiving and rallying his forces to try to build the new Babel (Babylon). He also knows that if he can keep God's people divided, he will make great headway in polarizing the people of the world against believers in Jesus. God is calling His people to be coming together in one accord. We are to focus on Jesus (**2 Peter 3:12-13**) which will make us unified and accomplishing God's purpose until the day of the coming of Jesus Christ.

God's "Perfect Will"?

Romans 8:28 (ESV) "And we know that for those who love God all things work together for good, for those who are called according to his purpose."

Have you ever wondered, "what if"? What if I'd made a different choice? What if I had chosen a different career, a different life, a different spouse? What if I had said "yes" instead of "no"? What if I had listened to the voice of the Holy Spirit when He was leading me to do something, but I didn't? What can I do to go back and make my life a "happily-ever-after" Hallmark movie? We used to hear a lot of teachings about God's "perfect will" verses His "permissive will". It was saying that there was a perfect plan for your life and you blew it, but God's grace will make the rest of your life somewhat tolerable in his "permissive will" because He loves you. Well, that's almost right, but, not quite. In fact, if you adhere to that, you will go the rest of your life thinking that you missed it. That's a miserable way to live.

Let me tell you the truth. There never was a "perfect will". Ever since the fall at Eden, the "happily-ever-after" moved to another place. That place is called the Kingdom of God, Heaven, Paradise, and so on. The good news is, Jesus said that we could experience the Kingdom of God while still on this earth.. In Matthew 6, He said to seek the Kingdom of God and His righteousness and all the things that matter in life would be added to us. A few verses later, He told us not to worry about tomorrow because today had enough going on. Lamentations 3:22-24 says, "²² *Through* the Lord's mercies we are not consumed, Because His compassions fail not. 23 *They are* new every morning; Great *is* Your faithfulness. 24 "The Lord *is* my portion," says my soul, "Therefore I hope in Him!" He also told us to spread this Kingdom to others Every day, God gives us the opportunity to be in His perfect will. We repent of our sins, allow the Holy Spirit to correct us and change us and make us more like Him. We become closer to that perfect Kingdom of God. Every day, we move closer to that perfect will. When Romans says "All things work together for good", it means that all the mistakes, bad choices, unfair treatment, tragedies, and all the other negative stuff, as well as all the good things, right choices, successes, etc., are used by God to develop us into what He intended us to be. God's grace takes the good, the bad, and the ugly, and replaces it with Himself.

So, the next time the devil tries to say you failed, just say, "That's right, I did. But it's all been redeemed. Just ask Jesus. He did it for me." Then get excited about who God is making you into!

Grasshopper or Overcomer?

Numbers 13:30 (NKJV)
"³⁰ Then Caleb quieted the people before Moses, and said, "Let us go up at once and take possession, for we are well able to overcome it.""

Numbers 13:33
³³ There we saw the giants (the descendants of Anak came from the giants); and we were like grasshoppers in our own sight, and so we were in their sight."

Joshua and Caleb went to the same places and saw the same things as the other ten representatives of the other tribes of Israel. Joshua and Caleb were looking up at the God who miraculously delivered them from the Egyptians and provided for them. The others were looking at the circumstances through the eyes of the flesh, not the Spirit. They depended on their feelings, not faith. They trusted their "gut" while Joshua and Caleb trusted God's Word. He had already told them that He would give them the land. If you see yourself as a grasshopper, so will the enemy. If you see yourself as a child of God, so will the enemy. That's why **James 4:7** says "Submit yourselves to God, resist the devil, and he will flee from you." The key is submitting yourself to God. Looking up at His kingdom and remembering His promises.

Colossians 3:2
"Set your mind on things above, not on things on the earth."

Grow and Bear Fruit

Jeremiah 17:7-9 (NKJV)
"Blessed *is* the man who trusts in the Lord,
And whose hope is the Lord.
[8] For he shall be like a tree planted by the waters,
Which spreads out its roots by the river,
And will not fear when heat comes;
But its leaf will be green,
And will not be anxious in the year of drought,
Nor will cease from yielding fruit."

Psalms 1:1-3
"1 Blessed *is* the man
Who walks not in the counsel of the ungodly,
Nor stands in the path of sinners,
Nor sits in the seat of the scornful;
[2] But his delight *is* in the law of the LORD,
And in His law he meditates day and night.
[3] He shall be like a tree
Planted by the ⌜rivers of water,
That brings forth its fruit in its season,
Whose leaf also shall not wither;
And whatever he does shall prosper."

Some Christians think that Christianity is only about God coming to earth, then being crucified and raised from the dead, because that's the only two messages they usually hear on Christmas and Easter. I'm not here to pick on the "Chreasters" though, I am saying that is what many believers live. There are now a lot more people who don't even know that much about Jesus. There are kids growing up who believe the Elf on the Shelf is just as real as Jesus and fictional characters elevated above Jesus because the kids hear more about them. Not just the kids; adults have their own set of idols, celebrities, teams, things, skills, etc. that are much more important to them. Tragically, I'm not talking about the secular society, I'm talking about people who identify themselves as Christians. God has called us for much more than that. If that's all there was to it, we would be better off if we were born again and immediately got taken up to Heaven.

But, there's a lot more to it than that. God wants us to be like that tree that bears much fruit (John 15). He wants us to GROW. He provides the Rivers of Living Water for us to draw from so our roots can go down deep. While we are here on this earth, we draw nearer to God every day, delighting ourselves in Him, meditating on Him, so we can grow and bear fruit. The fruit we bear is found in Galatians 5. Love, Joy, Peace, Patience, Gentleness, Kindness, Goodness, Self-Control, Faith and more. The result of that fruit will be other people who come to Christ and other believers who will grow stronger. We don't have to go through specialized training or disciplines to accomplish this or to make it better. We just learn to delight ourselves in the Lord, not in the scornful, not in agreement with sin, nor in the counsel of the ungodly. When we draw from God's Word, drink from His Spirit (the Living Water), and delight in Him, we will prosper in fulfilling what we were put here on earth to be, we will survive the droughts in our life and continue to thrive. He will show us what to do, take us where we need to go, and give us the power, knowledge, wisdom, and ability to do it.

Hananiah, Mishael, and Azariah

Daniel 3:17-18 (NKJV) "If this be so, our God whom we serve is able to deliver us from the burning fiery furnace, and he will deliver us out of your hand, O king. 18 But if not, be it known to you, O king, that we will not serve your gods or worship the golden image that you have set up."

Hananiah, Mishael, and Azariah was their Hebrew names. We know them better as Shadrach, Meshach, and Abed-Nego. They were put in an uncomfortable situation. Actually, it was more than that. It was a situation that directly demanded that they either confirm or deny everything that they lived, breathed, and believed.

We will have that same challenge during our lifetimes. In fact, in some way or form, we have that challenge on a daily basis. The result may not be life or death, but it will involve being "uncomfortable". How many conversations have we avoided, compromises with our faith we have made, because it was "uncomfortable"? Knowingly going along with what is obviously against God's Word and His will.

Hananiah, Mishael, and Azariah were beyond uncomfortable. They had been taken from their homelands, made eunuchs and slaves, separated from their families, stripped from their very identities, and lost their ambitions, hopes, and plans. Then they were told to bow before some ridiculous image and deny their God. The problem with that was, He was all they had left. They were stripped from every fleshly, earthly thing, and all they had left was their eternity and the One who made it and them.

Romans 6:4 says, "Therefore we were buried with Him through baptism into death, that just as Christ was raised from the dead by the glory of the Father, even so we also should walk in newness of life." **Galatians 2:20** says, "I have been crucified with Christ; it is no longer I who live, but Christ lives in me; and the life which I now live in the flesh I live by faith in the Son of God, who loved me and gave Himself for me."

The group, *Dogwood* (Steve and Annie Chapman and Ron Elder) used to sing one of my favorite lines, "You know, you don't have to suffer when you're dead…". If we've died with Christ, the old us is dead and the new one lives. Hananiah, Mishael, and Azariah said that their

God would deliver them, but "EVEN IF NOT…" they were still going to honor Him. If they fried, they would be alive in a moment with Him! They got thrown in the furnace, but "one who was like the Son of God" was with them and not a hair of their head was singed. Plus, they got to see the Savior whom they had been trusting in.

That same Savior is always with us. When we need to stand for what is right, He is with us. When we need to speak up and proclaim His Word, He is with us. When we need to share Him with a friend, family member, or enemy, He is with us. When we take that stand that will cause us to lose our job, friends, popularity, status, reputation, or (God forbid) make us uncomfortable, He is with us. Even if we lose these things, He is with us and that is far more important.

If you are uncomfortable talking about Jesus, raising your hands to worship, singing to Him, praying, being identified with Him, etc., just remember, life is not about being comfortable. Eternity without Jesus is very, very uncomfortable. Eternity with Him makes the word comfort seem insignificant.

Happiness

Matthew 6:33 (NKJV)
"But seek first the kingdom of God and His righteousness, and all these things shall be added to you."

The Declaration of Independence says that we have these "unalienable rights", "life, liberty, and the pursuit of happiness". Many folks spend all their lives seeking happiness and never find it. Some begin to find it, but it is never enough. Jay Gould, and American railroad magnate in the late 19ᵗʰ century was one of the richest men on earth. On his death bed, he was quoted as saying, "I suppose I am the most miserable man on earth". He had everything money could buy, but it didn't make him happy. Some say, "if only I'd win the Powerball, I'd be happy". The majority of lottery winners so far have spent it all and many are back where they started. Many try to find happiness through many means; favorite hobbies, travelling, education, their job, drugs, porn, sexual sin, popularity, prestige, power, even religion…, you get it. Most of these provide some temporary pleasure, but the end result is the same. Just like a sand castle, they are fun for a little while, then they all end. Most of them end you. Galatians 5 names a long list of these things as "the works of the works of the flesh". The end result is death. Then it talks about the fruit of the Holy Spirit: love, joy, peace, patience, gentleness, kindness, goodness, faithfulness, self-control. This sounds like happiness, right? The secret to happiness is walking with the Holy Spirit, or God, just like Adam and Eve did in the Garden.

Jesus said to seek the Kingdom of God first. Jeremiah 29:13 says, "And you will seek Me and find Me, when you search for Me with all your heart..". Proverbs 8:35 says, "For whoever finds me finds life, And obtains favor from the Lord;". Jesus said in John 10:10, "The thief does not come except to steal, and to kill, and to destroy. I have come that they may have life, and that they may have it more abundantly." Adam and Eve walked with God in the Garden (this was God in "man" form, so you can picture Him as Jesus). Everything was perfect and unhappiness was unheard of until they quit walking with Him. Ever since then, it has been our task to seek Him and His Kingdom to return to that place of happiness. So, the secret to happiness is not to seek happiness, but to seek the Lord and He will add the happiness "unto you". The way to do it is to let go of your old self, sin, desires, ambitions, ego… all of it. Let it be crucified with Christ (put to death) by confessing and repenting of your sins, and believe that God raised Jesus from the dead and that He lives today. Then ask Him to come into you, to literally come inside of you and take over your life. Then you will be happy.

Have You Met Him?

Job 42:5 (ESV) "I had heard of you by the hearing of the ear, but now my eye sees you;"

Recently, I visited to a man who was in his mid-80s who was recovering from an illness. I had visited him many times and always enjoyed it because he is very interesting, friendly, and always has good stories to tell. He is also a very good and kind man who was raised in church and has always gone when he could. We were enjoying visiting with each other and I was getting ready to pray with him and leave. Right before that, I felt a check in my spirit and knew the Holy Spirit wanted me to ask him if he had ever had a personal encounter with the Lord. I asked him if he remembered a specific time when he was saved. He began to tell me where he went to church as a child and all the different places he had gone over the years. Then he started to tell me what he believed and that he hoped he was going to Heaven.

I told my friend how I also was raised in church, but when I was almost 16 years old, I realized sin had control of my life and I wasn't ready to go to Heaven. I told him how many of my friends were telling me about their salvation experience and how they were praying that I would experience it too. Not long after that, I went to a Sunday night youth revival and the preacher told the graphic details of what Jesus went through for us when He was whipped and crucified and how He paid for our sins and took our place. He gave the invitation and I went to the altar and met Him for the first time. That was 52 years ago and my life has never been the same since then. I also told him how Billy Graham said that many people miss Heaven by 18 inches; the distance between the head and the heart.

Next, I told him about a lady who was a relative from Kentucky. She also was heavily involved in church work; she had even helped start a new church in her town. She traveled all over the world doing mission work. I was surprised one day when she called me and told me that she wanted me to come and pray with her. When I got there she told me that she felt that she had known God for 40 years, but she didn't know Jesus. I prayed with her and she asked Jesus to be her Lord and Savior. She was 94 years old! Her life literally changed for the next four years until she went home to be with Him at 98.

After that, my friend asked me if I would mind praying with him He asked Jesus to forgive him for his sins and be his Savior. On the way home, I wondered how many people there were out there who knew about God or Jesus, but didn't know Him. How many people are missing Heaven by 18 inches? Pray first, then ask people if they have met Him. More than that, make sure you've had that encounter with Him.

He Made Us, Not the Other Way Around

Psalm 100:3 (ESV) "Know that the Lord, he is God!
It is he who made us, and we are his;
we are his people, and the sheep of his pasture."

It's ok to ask God a question, but not to question God. It is 100% guaranteed that something will happen during your life that God allows to happen that you do not understand or agree with. It is pretty likely that this will happen this week or even today. The closer we grow in our relationship to Jesus, the more we understand that He has our lives under control if we submit them to Him. That's called letting Jesus be Lord of our lives. I recently had a question about why something happened. It included free-will and all sorts of things that come up in theological questions. I told God that I wasn't questioning Him (He already knew that), I just wanted to understand. To my surprise (I know, duh), the Holy Spirit explained it to me. It was one of those "downloads" that just dropped the understanding down in my spirit where I just knew in a second what could have taken hours to explain in words. It all boiled down to "that's who He is and that's how He made it".

So many people want to question God, defy Him, shake their fist at Him (and yes, He's big enough to handle it), but they forget Who made who. He made us. Man-made religion creates a god. When we have a true, living relationship with Him, we realize that He created us; that we are His sheep. If we trust in Him, He will lead us into His pastures, watch over us, restore us, provide for us, love us, and make us part of Him, and Him a part of us. Trusting Him means that when something happens, whether or not we understand it, we just scoot closer to Him and walk as closely to Him as possible. It's really freeing to let our Maker be in control.

He Set Them In the Firmament

Genesis 1:16 (NKJV) "Then God made two great lights: the greater light to rule the day, and the lesser light to rule the night. *He made* the stars also. ¹⁷ God set them in the firmament of the heavens to give light on the earth, ¹⁸ and to rule over the day and over the night, and to divide the light from the darkness. And God saw that *it was* good. ¹⁹ So the evening and the morning were the fourth day."

Today, I was sitting in a chair out in my yard, watching the eclipse. The wind began to blow, the light was dimmer, the birds were singing and gliding over, and it became quiet in that way that happens when you are experiencing the Kingdom of God. I looked up and saw the tops of the trees swaying back and forth which took me back to a moment in 2011. My dad had just died and I was having a hard time with it. I was the one who had found him and I couldn't get that image out of my head. We had recently had the reassuring conversation where he knew he was ready to go to Heaven because he believed on Jesus. I had no reason to doubt, but the enemy tried to instill that fear. Three days later, I was up early in the morning, walking the dog and praying, and I saw the tops of the same trees I was looking at today. They were swaying in the wind and there was that same surreal feeling. I felt I was "in the Spirit" as John described in Revelation 1. The trees I was looking at became much taller and were still swaying and I saw my dad as a young man around 18 or 20 years old looking up at awe at the trees and running with his arms hanging straight down like I used to see him run when he was much younger. At that point, I knew I saw him in Heaven and that he was full of awe and joy.

Then, I came back to the realization of where I was today, looking at the moon, blocking out most of the sun. You know, there are a lot of things going on now; celestial, mystical, prophetic, supernatural, natural, and the eclipse was one of them. Scriptures like Matthew 24, Mark 13, Luke 17 and 21, and many other books in the Bible say that there will be signs in the Heavenlies in the last days. But this eclipse doesn't point to any certain day or hour when the Son of Man will return. What it does point to though is that we have a Creator that placed everything in a perfect balance and it was created for His pleasure as well as for ourselves. How can anyone believe that the moon was accidentally, just the right size, placed at the right distance of orbit to block out precisely the exact amount of the sun where you can actually see only its corona? Or how about, the distance, size, orbit and speed of the moon around the earth being at the perfect balance to where if the speed or distance was off by less than 1%, would either fly off into space or crash onto the earth. The same with the earth orbiting the sun, and so on. You can find that perfect balance in the molecules, atoms, systems in our body, levels of sunlight, water, oxygen and other gases, etc. on earth to support life. Volumes of books are filled with these facts that go much deeper.

The point of all this is, this same God, knows all the things going on in your life, your past, your future, and what is going on now. He will make all things work together for good if you trust Him. He has a divine balance, a calling, a plan for your life. No matter what is going on in your life, Jesus, the Creator (John 1, Colossians 1:15-17) lives inside of you if you have surrendered your life to Him. He is real. He is interested in what it going on in your life and He loves you. Trust Him!

He Stops the Storm

Psalm 107:28-29 (NKJV)
"Then they cry out to the Lord in their trouble,
And He brings them out of their distresses.
29 He calms the storm,
So that its waves are still."

Mark 3:37 "And a great windstorm arose, and the waves beat into the boat, so that it was already filling. 38 But He was in the stern, asleep on a pillow. And they awoke Him and said to Him, "Teacher, do You not care that we are perishing?"
39 Then He arose and rebuked the wind, and said to the sea, "Peace, be still!" And the wind ceased and there was a great calm."

Jesus, again, demonstrated that He was the One longed for in the songs and prophecies in the Old Testament. The disciples were literally in trouble, literally cried out, and Jesus literally calmed the storm and made the waves become still. Was this a prophecy fulfilled? Yes. But it was more. It showed who God is and that He and Jesus are one. We broke the relationship with Him by unbelief and sin. He made it where we can reunite into that fellowship with Him by calling to Him and believing. Many times, it has to be when we are in times of distress, but, yes, He is able to speak and make the storm stop, and yes, He was there all the time. He can make the storm stop in your life. Call out to Him, He is there.

He Who Now Restrains

I believe the Lord showed me something several years ago about the assumption that the Holy Spirit would be "taken out of the world" based on 2 Thessalonians 2 because He is restraining the Antichrist from being revealed. I believe it is a false assumption.

In **2 Thessalonians 2:7-9 (NKJV)** is says, "For the mystery of lawlessness is already at work; only He who now restrains *will do so* until He is taken out of the way. ⁸ And then the lawless one will be revealed, whom the Lord will consume with the breath of His mouth and destroy with the brightness of His coming." Notice the little letter by the word "He". The footnote shows that it should be a small "he".

The assumption is that the Holy Spirit will be taken out of the world and the Beast or Lawless One will finally be revealed. All the people who may come to Christ will be doing so on their own knowledge of the Word of God without the Holy Spirit.

First, the Holy Spirit is God. He is omnipresent. He is not a force or thing that can be removed. Since He is God, no one "removes" Him from anywhere. Second, people don't come to Jesus Christ without being drawn by the Holy Spirit. Thirdly, the original text uses a small case "h" for "he", denoting that it is someone besides God.

One day I was reading Daniel and I got to the final chapter, 12. **Daniel 12:1** says:

> ""At that time **Michael** shall stand up,
> The great prince who stands *watch* over the sons of your people;
> And there shall be a time of trouble,
> Such as never was since there was a nation,
> *Even* to that time.
> And at that time your people shall be delivered,
> Every one who is found written in the book.

Some versions say Michael shall arise. Michael has been the one guarding and fighting for Israel earlier in Daniel and other places. The time of trouble, or Great Tribulation starts as soon as Michael arises, and all of God's people will be delivered (possibly raptured) also at that time. I believe it will be Michael who tosses the Beast and False Prophet live in the Lake of Fire, seals Satan in the bottomless pit for 1000 years, and finally throws him in the Lake of Fire.

With his authority and based on Daniel 12, I believe that the "one who restrains" is Michael the archangel, not the Holy Spirit.

Heavenly Minded

Colossians 3:1-4 (NKJV)

"If then you were raised with Christ, seek those things which are above, where Christ is, sitting at the right hand of God. 2 Set your mind on things above, not on things on the earth. 3 For you died, and your life is hidden with Christ in God. 4 When Christ who is our life appears, then you also will appear with Him in glory."

Have you heard the old adage, "They are so heavenly minded that they are no earthly good"? I was trying to imagine what the earth might be like if everyone was heavenly minded. You know, seeking first, the Kingdom of God and its righteousness. There would be no hate, war, lying, stealing, killing. We would be helping each other and making sure no one would be without. That's because when we have our minds set on the Kingdom of God, we are connecting to it. We are allowing it to flow through us to everyone around us.

This passage says our lives will be "hidden in Christ." We will be wrapped in Him and He will continue His mission here through us until He returns. Then it says we will "appear with Him in glory."

Have you noticed that everything in this fallen world distracts us from Him? If we focus on the darkness, evil, our own desires, what others do or have done, etc., our eyes are not on Jesus. The world continues to develop new ways to distract us, just in case we get bored. We have every kind of technology designing scenarios to direct our imaginations in a way that the demonic enemies have designed. Whether movies, shows, video games, music, or social media, someone tries to guide our thinking in the wrong direction. I've noticed that almost no one knows how to make a good movie anymore. You can't tell the "good guy" from the "bad guy". They don't have happy endings. You don't get good messages from many of them when it is over. They are filled with confusion, frustration, and chaos. I say "their imagination well has gone dry".

Thankfully, we don't have to live in that world. That is why God made His Kingdom available to us now by Christ living in us. By looking to His Kingdom, the Holy Spirit joins with our spirit and mind and lets us see the goodness of God. If you seem overwhelmed with the illusions and delusions of the world, look up above it; rise up into the Kingdom of God. It says "seek things above...", verse 2 says "set your mind on things above". That part is our decision. We need to make it constantly.

Hindrance Is Not Defeat, Just Winning God's Way

1 Thessalonians 2:18 (NKJV) "Therefore we wanted to come to you—even I, Paul, time and again—but Satan hindered us. ¹⁹ For what *is* our hope, or joy, or crown of rejoicing? *Is it* not even you in the presence of our Lord Jesus Christ at His coming? ²⁰ For you are our glory and joy."

When God reveals part of His plan to us, often, our first reaction is to get excited and start figuring out how we are going to accomplish it (at least I do). I have discovered that whenever I do that, it inevitably happens another way. God doesn't tell us to do something and then hands it to us to do. He gives us something that is extremely difficult or even impossible to do on our own so we and He can do it together. (**Philippians 4:13** "I can do all things through Christ who strengthens me.")

When you see a detour sign, the first reaction is usually negative. You had planned to go that way, you set your GPS to go that way and it had not figured in that detour yet. You are going to be late! You get to the meeting or appointment and everything was ok, or not. I missed a Dr.'s appointment once because of that very reason. There was a detour and even though I had left early, I was ten minutes late. I called ahead and told them and it seemed to be ok. I got there and the receptionist informed me that I would have to reschedule because I was actually 12 minutes late and they only allowed 10. She said it was because it would slow down the schedule because it overlapped with the other appointments. I looked around the waiting room and I was the only one there. I had taken off work that day for that appointment. I had driven twenty miles to get there. I, calmly (with the Lord's help), told her not to reschedule me because I would not be back. Looking back at that, I realized that it was a God moment, a hindrance, but I remembered Romans 8:28 and I knew that it was going to work together for good because I loved God and I was called according to His purpose. What I didn't know was His plan. The obvious good result is, because of that, for the last 15 years, I have been going to a great doctor who is only about ten miles from me. He listens to me and has always given me the right treatment. Once, he picked up on symptoms that led to having my gall bladder removed and was probably life-saving. There are other good results that I may never know here on this earth. Maybe I got to (or still will have the opportunity to) influence someone towards knowing Christ or something along those lines.

The point is, the rest of Paul's story turned out like this for the Thessalonians: **1 Thessalonians 3:1** "Therefore, when we could no longer endure it, we thought it good to be left in Athens alone, [2] and sent Timothy, our brother and minister of God, and our fellow laborer in the gospel of Christ, to establish you and encourage you concerning your faith… Paul and his entourage were literally detained, but Timothy became their dynamic, young pastor and God used him mightily there.

God isn't there to make things go our way. He teaches us to let Him lead us His way." Amen

His Benefits

Psalms 103:1 (NKJV) "Bless the LORD, O my soul;
And all that is within me, *bless* His holy name!
[2] Bless the LORD, O my soul,
And forget not all His benefits:
[3] Who forgives all your iniquities,
Who heals all your diseases,
[4] Who redeems your life from destruction,
Who crowns you with lovingkindness and tender mercies,
[5] Who satisfies your mouth with good *things,*
So that your youth is renewed like the eagle's."

Have you ever gotten a job and were so glad that you finally knew that you were going to be able to pay the bills, buy groceries, and stay in your house? Then as you were being told about the details, they began to describe the job benefits that you didn't even know were included. What an extra blessing. I remember a time in my life during the 70s and 80s when it was hard to find a job, period. If you did, it would barely be enough to pay the bills and benefits were not expected. I was just thankful to have a job. When I would find out that it had extra benefits; insurance, bonuses, vacations, etc., it made me feel as if the employer actually valued having me be with them.

In the Kingdom of God, when we believe and receive, we are thankful to have eternal life. We can finally go through life and not wonder if we are going to go the Heaven or Hell. What a relief! But in Psalms 103, David is blessing the Lord with all his might just because He is Lord! David knows Him as Lord, King, Friend, etc. and he is praising Yahweh with all of his soul. But then, he says, "Forget not all His benefits". Just knowing Jesus gives us eternal life, but along with that, He forgives all our sins, He heals our diseases, He redeems the mess we made of our lives, He gives us His love and mercy and gives us the ability to give it to others, He provides our needs, He renews our youth, and He does much, much, more. Many have tried to use the benefits to "sell" Jesus, but that's not how it works. It reminds me of the old bumper sticker that says "Try Jesus". You don't try Jesus. You dive in, all or nothing. Once you do, you get all that He has to offer, including His benefits. The main thing is, we do not become a believer and follower of Jesus Christ so we can have eternal life, we do it because He is Lord. We were created to know Him, worship Him, and fellowship with Him. Eternal life, just like all the other things, is a benefit. Bless the Lord!

I Knew You

Jeremiah 1:5 (NKJV)"Before I formed you in the womb I knew you; Before you were born I sanctified you; I ordained you a prophet to the nations."

I Never Knew You

Matthew 7:21

"And then I will declare to them, 'I never knew you; depart from Me, you who practice lawlessness!'

How can this be? How can God know some before they are born and never have known others? People have tried to figure this out from our limited, time-line perspective and don't think about it from God's eternal viewpoint. We don't really have a "present" where we live because we see everything from this perspective. What I am about to type is the future and now that I've typed it, it is past. Where is the present? That's where God lives. He is the Alpha and Omega, the beginning and the end. He doesn't have to predict or reminisce. He sees it all. **Romans 8:29** says, "For whom He foreknew, He also predestined to be conformed to the image of His Son, that He might be the firstborn among many brethren." He knows if we are going to say yes or no; if we are going to believe or not, and if we will obey or not.

I remember several instances when I was a very young child. I would talk to God and it was like He was right there. I even remember some things that He showed me that I couldn't explain in words (and I still can't). I knew that He knew me. When I was fifteen, the old, rebellious nature had risen up in me to where it was taking over who I was. Yet, the One who knew me kept letting me stumble across things in my path that reminded me of Him. He had people praying for me and friends sharing their experience with me, but most of all, His Spirit was stirring inside of me. Then, in January of 1971, I came back to the One who knew me. I surrendered my life to Jesus Christ and let Him take over. He washed me clean from sin and came inside of me to live with me as close as one could possibly get.

Now, every day that I let Him, He makes me into His image. Some days I let Him do it more than others. Those are the days I try to do it myself, or the days I forget how close He is in every situation. But like Jeremiah, He has plans for me. He has plans for you. He knew exactly what you were going to be before you were born because He is the One making you into that very thing. Here is more good news: He knew how messed up you were going to be. He took every goof-up, wrong choice, sin, and even those things that we think we will never get over, and, not only forgave them, He used all of them to make us into what we are now. He turned all the bad situations into something good. That's what Romans 8:28 means when it says that "all things work together for good for those who are in Christ and are called according to His purpose." That's because we are in Christ Jesus now and there is nothing bad in Him. That is what the Bible is talking about when it mentions the name, Redeemer 22 times. He took our place and paid the price for us and made everything as if we had never sinned. That is what the Redeemer does. **Isaiah 47:4** As for our Redeemer, the Lord of hosts is His name, The Holy One of Israel.

I Know

Job 19:25 (ESV) "For I know that my Redeemer lives, and at the last he will stand upon the earth.

One of my favorite quotes from my former pastor and mentor, Dr. J.T. Parish was, "The man with the experience is not at the mercy of the man with the argument". When you have "been there, done that", seen it, tasted it, etc., no one can convince you otherwise. Another thing Bro. Parish used to say was, that when God shows you something, "you know it down in your knower".

I've had people try to convince me that God wasn't real, that miracles didn't happen, that the Bible wasn't true, and that God didn't talk to you today. Other than irritating me for wasting my time, they didn't have any effect on me. That's because I had just spent time with the Lord and heard the Holy Spirit speaking to me in my spirit, or seen something that day that only God could have done. They might as well have told me that my mother wasn't real, she was just a figment of my imagination that I believed because I had been conditioned to believe in her all my life. Something that may seem shocking is that most of that didn't come from people you would consider "heathen", but from religious people. I have had professors in Christian colleges, theologians, and even pastors try to talk me out of my faith. I know people who were convinced by them and quit believing. I didn't quit because I already knew Him. I didn't "try" Jesus, I let Him come inside of me. I let Him remake me. I gave Him my old self so it could be crucified with Him and put to death, then the new me was reborn when the Holy Spirit came in and brought me to life. So, no; I know that my Redeemer lives!

Job had been stripped of literally everything. His possessions, his children, his health, all friends, everything that could be considered worth living for. The only thing he had left was the One who created him. That was the only thing that mattered. That is the only thing that matters in our life. Jesus said to seek that (the Kingdom of God) first, and all the other things would be added (**Matt. 6:33**). When people, circumstances, the devil, or anything else might try to strip you of the things in life that might seem important, remember, you have the One who said "I will never leave you nor forsake you." (**Hebrews 13:5**). If you know Him, you know this. If you haven't asked Jesus in yet, do it today.

I Pity the Fool

Psalms 14:1 (NKJV) "The fool has said in his heart, "*There is* no God. "They are corrupt, They have done abominable works,

There is none who does good."

Many times, I would get to play the role of the apologist arguing with unbelievers, agnostics, and atheists. Most of them would come across as sounding "intellectual", but they would actually have a small arsenal of information from one or two books they read to back up their beliefs. Some would only have watched a pseudo-documentary or listened to a podcast. I can only remember one who actually read the whole Bible. Most of them were hoping that they could prove there was no God because they either had a "beef" with God over something that happened in their lives, or they were living a lifestyle that was unacceptable according to Christian beliefs. I have actually talked to a couple of "sincere atheists" or agnostics who couldn't believe in God based upon what they knew at the time. When they saw that I was sincere and that it had changed my life, they began to soften and ask questions that showed they were really seeking.

Some names you might recognize did the same thing. They were atheists or agnostics who actually tried to disprove God, and the more they investigated, the more proof there was that there actually is a God. C.S. Lewis, Joy Davidman-C.S. Lewis' wife, Lee Strobel, Kirk Cameron, singer- Keith Green, William J. Murray III (son of Madelyn Murray O'Hare), Aleksandr Solzhenitsyn, Alister McGrath – biochemist and Christian theologian, Howard Storm –Atheist Professor whose Near-death Experience In Hell Changed led him to Jesus Christ, Jim Warner Wallace – was a Cold-Case homicide detective who worked for the LAPD, and many, many, more. In each of these cases, after making an honest effort to dig and look into the facts, they came out believing. Some of these names mentioned became the most prominent defenders of the faith after trying to destroy it.

One of the names I haven't mentioned yet is a fellow named Saul who was so diligent in his attempt to destroy Christianity that he put believers in prison and had some put to death. When he finally met Jesus on the road to Damascus, he showed us what a true "180 degree" repentance was all about. After that when his name was changed to Paul, he was hunted, imprisoned, beaten, stoned, shipwrecked, and finally beheaded for the faith. Dr. J.T. Parish, my pastor and mentor in the 80s, used to say, "the man with the experience is not at the mercy of the man with the argument". Once you have experienced Jesus, literally meeting Him, receiving Him inside of you, and walking with Him daily, you can no longer be convinced that He does not exist. Those who don't believe have never met Him. My question to them is, if He isn't real, then why go to all the trouble of convincing others? I believe the real answer is, those who most vehemently oppose Him know He is real. Their thought processes are influenced by something else who they say they don't believe in, demons. Another practical reason is, when you are doing something wrong, if you can get others to agree with you, you can say it must not be wrong. I believe the true atheist doesn't see the need to make the effort to try to convince others. The activist-atheist is the person who really has a beef with God over something that went wrong in their life or is living a lifestyle that they know God wouldn't approve of and they don't want to change.

Here's the bottom line. Every human being is going to have periods during their lives when something happens that they have no control over. There will be a time when they cannot make it, even with help from others. They will need help from God. (Matthew 19:26

But Jesus looked at them and said to them, "With men this is impossible, but with God all things are possible."). The universal encounter with this is when it is time to leave this body and cross into eternity. No one will be able to have eternal life without God's help. That is the ultimate goal that Satan has for the atheist, to deceive them until that day, believing something that he didn't even believe. (James 2:19- You believe that there is one God. You do well. Even the demons believe—and tremble!)

The big question I have to the unbeliever is, why is it so hard for you to believe? You can pretend that you are at a level of intellect above everyone else (which is a normal posture for the doubter). Yet the Bible calls you a fool. Why? Well, among millions of things, most people can look around them and see God's handiwork, delicate balance of nature, times of protection and provision, and feel and sense His presence. (2 Corinthians 4:3-4-3 But even if our gospel is veiled, it is veiled to those who are perishing, whose minds the god of this age has blinded, who do not believe, lest the light of the gospel of the glory of Christ, who is the image of God, should shine on them.) Pray that God will remove the blinders and let you see His glorious light!

John 8:12 Then Jesus spoke to them again, saying, "I am the light of the world. He who follows Me shall not walk in darkness, but have the light of life."

I Shall Not Be Moved

Psalms 62:1 (NKJV) starts out with:
"Truly my soul silently *waits* for God;
From Him *comes* my salvation.
² He only *is* my rock and my salvation;
He is my defense;
I shall not be greatly moved."

I saw where David said, "I shall not be greatly moved." I thought, "Okay, that makes sense. We are going through things in life that shake us, and even intentionally try to remove us from our firm foundation. In **Deuteronomy 32:15**, Deborah sings, ""… Then he forsook God who made him, And scornfully esteemed the Rock of his salvation." We have those who will directly challenge our faith and what God has called us to do, but they are really challenging God himself. They will always be defeated. But when the storm is over, our feet are planted on the Solid Rock (**2 Samuel 22:47, Matthew 7:24**) and we are still standing. That sums up most of the last 53 years of my Christian walk. Had I not had the Rock, Jesus, to stand upon, I would have been blown away a long time ago.

But then, something else caught my eye. Two verses down, it says, "⁵ My soul, wait silently for God alone, For my expectation *is* from Him. ⁶ He only *is* my rock and my salvation; *He is* my defense;
I shall not be moved.

It changed from, "I shall not be greatly moved, to I shall not be moved." I realized that during the time I was going through the tumult, like when I fall or get hurt, I check myself out and nothing seems to be broken, then I get up and say, "I guess I wasn't hurt that bad." Then I realize that, other than a bruise or two, I wasn't damaged at all. We will go through a times when we are shaken, but after each time, we look down and see that we are still standing on that Rock and each time, we realize that we are actually part of that Rock. It is not just supporting us, it IS us. Jesus literally lives inside of us (**Colossians 1:27**). He is not just supporting us, not just beside us, not our co-pilot, He is in us and we are one. These storms, trials, and difficult times are inevitable because we live in a fallen world and there is a devil, but we have already won the war, because He has already won it. And we are in Him, and He in us. Hallelujah!

"I"

The Personality of Satan

Isaiah 14:12 (NKJV) "How you are fallen from heaven,
O Lucifer, son of the morning!
How you are cut down to the ground,
You who weakened the nations!
[13] For you have said in your heart:
'I ...will ascend into heaven,
I ...will exalt my throne above the stars of God;
I ...will also sit on the mount of the congregation
On the farthest sides of the north;
[14] I ...will ascend above the heights of the clouds,
I ...will... be... like... the Most High.'
[15] Yet you shall be brought down to Sheol,
To the lowest depths of the Pit."

Isaiah starts this chapter by prophesying the fate of the King of Babylon, then he shifts to the spirit behind the ruler of Babylon, Lucifer. He prophesies what is later described in Revelation; the fall of Satan (Rev. 20). In this segment in Isaiah 14, it tells what made Lucifer fall. One word, one letter... "I". "I will... ascend into heaven", "I will make my throne above the stars of God", "I will rule over the congregation of the earth", "I will ascend above the clouds, and I will be like the Most High." He took his eyes off of God and His glory, and His beauty, and His love, etc., and he turned them upon himself. That is why he fell.

People, before they are reborn, naturally have their eyes turned toward themselves. That is the fallen nature, inherited when Satan talked Eve and Adam into doubting God's Word, motives, and nature. He passed on his nature to them, now to us, through unbelief, and then sin. When our spirit is reborn and united with God's Spirit, we are turned back to focusing on God, then others, and last, ourselves. The temptation that Satan brings daily, is to return our focus back to our old selves. If we allow him to do that, he wins, but he can't if we are in Christ Jesus. Romans 8:1 says, "Therefore there is no condemnation for those who are in Christ Jesus, (the original text leaves off the next part) who walk not after the flesh, but after the Spirit." First, we are IN Christ Jesus. We are surrounded by Him, we are walking with Him. Satan cannot get past Him. Now, for the part where we listen to the Spirit instead of the flesh. That is where we train ourselves to stop serving the old self and putting "I" first. When I am in Christ, I am His. I think about Him, serve Him, and live for Him. "I" has been crucified with Him. The reborn "me" has risen with Him and been transformed into one who lives to serve Him and others.

The world if full of "I" people who do not understand the new nature given us by Jesus. That is why they think we are crazy; we are not still serving self. 2 Timothy 3 describes them like this: "But know this, that in the last days perilous times will come: ² For men will be lovers of themselves, lovers of money, boasters, proud, blasphemers, disobedient to parents, unthankful, unholy, ³ unloving, unforgiving, slanderers, without self-control, brutal, despisers of good, ⁴ traitors, headstrong, haughty, lovers of pleasure rather than lovers of God, ⁵ having a form of godliness but denying its power. And from such people turn away!"

This will continue to increase until the Lord returns. Also, those will those increase who are set free from serving self (and the devil), because they have taken "I" off the throne of their hearts and put Jesus there. It is vital that we walk in the Spirit, that we seek His presence, every day. That is what He called us to do.

In Everything Give Thanks

---

1 Thessalonians 5:18 (NKJV)
"In everything give thanks; for this is the will of God in Christ Jesus for you.
Everything? The key here is IN everything. Thankfulness is the norm in the Kingdom of God."

Psalm 100:4 says, "Enter into His gates with thanksgiving, And into His courts with praise. Be thankful to Him, and bless His name."

The very essence of the atmosphere in Heaven is thankfulness. You can't even enter the front yard without thanksgiving. Once you see, even just a glimpse of His Kingdom, you are thankful for His mercy, His grace, His love. Then once you step on His front porch, it all turns into praise.

Listen closely to this: when we are giving thanks, we are bypassing the situations we see with our eyes and feel with our skin and hear with our ears, and even imagine in our heads. We are entering by faith into that Kingdom where the very air reverberates with thankfulness. Giving thanks is simply thanking Him that when He lives in us, He brought us out of this fallen realm into His Kingdom of Light. Thank you Lord that you loved me enough to do that and you love me enough to continue doing that!

IN HIM

Acts 17:28 (NKJV) "For in Him we live and move and have our being, as also some of your own poets have said, 'For we are also His offspring.'"

In HIM. In JESUS. In no other place is there life for the believer; no other place can we even make a move or breathe. Our very essence and being is in Him. A person who hasn't met Jesus yet may find that concept as strange, but when you become "in Him", by believing and immersing yourself in Him, you realize there is no other place you'd rather be. In Ephesians 1, it says that He has made known to us the mystery of His will (vs. 9), that He would gather together as one all things "in Christ", both things which are in Heaven and in earth- "in Him"(vs. 10). In fact, the phrases "in Him", "in Christ", "in the Beloved", are mentioned 14 times in that one chapter. That is the "mystery" or secret of Christianity. It is not a belief system, it is a state of being. It literally transforms us, brings us to life, activates us, by killing the old sinful self and making it alive again by being in Him.

I have given this example many times in sermons. I would take a piece of paper with writing or scribbling on it in one hand and the Bible in the other hand. The piece of paper is us. The writing is sin. We cannot be in God's presence nor in His kingdom with our sinful or dirty garments so God cannot look at us. The Bible represents Jesus Christ who knew no sin. When we, by faith, let our old selves die and be buried in Him, we are "in Christ". I would put the piece of paper in the Bible and close it. Now when we look for the piece of paper, we only see the Bible. When God looks at us, He only sees His Son. That is the secret. That is the only place I want to be.

In the Cleft of the Rock

Exodus 33:20 (NKJV) "But He said, "You cannot see My face; for no man shall see Me, and live." ²¹ And the Lᴏʀᴅ said, "Here is a place by Me, and you shall stand on the rock. ²² So it shall be, while My glory passes by, that I will put you in the cleft of the rock, and will cover you with My hand while I pass by."

God told Moses that He wanted him to be with Him and experience His glory. There was one problem though. Moses was not able to survive in God's full glory. Moses was still living in the old sinful flesh that was under the curse of death through Adam. So God says, "Here… stand on this *Rock*…while I put you in the cleft of the *Rock*." (I emphasized who the Rock was with the capital R). God put His hand over the rock until He passed by. Now, if you are in this Rock (Psalms 62:2 He only is my rock and my salvation; He is my defense; I shall not be greatly moved), and standing on it, you can draw near to God and His glory. When we believe on Jesus, the Rock of our salvation, we are in the cleft of the Rock. We are literally *in Christ* (2 Corinthians 5:17). Because the Rock can withstand the glory of God, we are safe to be in the very presence of God the Father. I used to think of being in that Rock is what protected us from the attacks of the devil, but the protection actually comes from being near God and all His glory. Being in Jesus allows us to be in the presence of the Father without fear; just love.

In The Morning

Psalm 30:5 (NKJV)

"For His anger is but for a moment, His favor is for life; Weeping may endure for a night, But joy comes in the morning."

Thank God for morning! I can't number the days that I went to bed with a burden of sorrow, worry, guilt, fear, confusion, a feeling of no answers and no way out. Then, in the morning, the problem was not gone, but there was a new hope. The sun came up, and I remembered the One who created the morning is the One who has me and my problem in His hand. The problem didn't change. I just handed it to the God who created the universe in six days. Each new phase of the creation started with "so the evening and the morning". Each new part of His creation started in "the morning". **Psalms 5:3** says, "My voice You shall hear in the morning, O Lord; In the morning I will direct *it* to You, And I will look up." Let's direct it to Jesus, then look up!

Infinite

Psalms 147:3 (NKJV) "He heals the brokenhearted
And binds up their wounds.
⁴ He counts the number of the stars;
He calls them all by name.
⁵ Great *is* our Lord, and mighty in power;
His understanding *is* infinite."

Ephesians 3:20 "Now to Him who is able to do exceedingly abundantly above all that we ask or think, according to the power that works in us."

Whenever I think of **Ephesians 3:20**, I always think, "He is able to do above all that we ask or think", then I stretch my imagination as far as I can. Then I think, "…able to do abundantly above…", and I try to stretch my imagination even farther. Then I think, "…EXCEEDINGLY, abundantly, above all that we ask or think", and I just let it go and realize that there is no limit to what God can do. **Psalms 147:4** helps with that a little. "He counts the number of stars;" (and if that isn't enough to blow your mind) "He CALLS THEM BY NAME"! I shouldn't be so surprised because He made them all, but we can't even begin to count them. I used to hear statements like, "There are a hundred million galaxies, and ours has 200 million stars". I always thought, "if the universe is infinite, how does anyone know?" Then a few years later you would hear, "There are 200 million galaxies in the universe", and so on. The truth is, no one but God and those in His eternal kingdom know. The greater truth is, it is exceedingly, abundantly, beyond our imagination.

The greatest truth is, He who named all the stars, "heals the brokenhearted and binds up their wounds"! When you need help from God, and ask Jesus to help, remember that He is the one who knows the names of all the stars. He created each one. He created you. His love for you is just as infinite as everything else about Him. Don't be afraid to ask.

Insight

Daniel 12:3 (NASB) "And those who have insight will shine like the glow of the expanse of heaven, and those who lead the many to righteousness, like the stars forever and ever."

Where the word, "wisdom" is used in most versions in this verse, the New American Standard Bible uses the word, "insight". They both mean the same thing, but the word "wisdom" can be looked at as regular, worldly wisdom, that you might get from experience, study, etc. The word "insight" implies that it was revealed to you. This verse is talking about the last of the last days. Those who have God's insight, or those led by the Holy Spirit, will have a countenance about them that the world doesn't understand. It will draw many out of darkness into His marvelous light. Our job, calling, passion, will be to lead many to righteousness. Acts 2 and Joel 2 talk about this time when God will pour His Spirit out upon all flesh, miracles will take place, young people will see visions and prophesy, old people will have revelations and dreams; they will be receiving insight. The purpose of this outpouring is to bring as many out of darkness into the light as possible before Jesus appears. Over the last few years, I have seen and felt this coming, over the last few months, I have begun to see it manifest all around me as well as in my life. More people are receptive to coming to Jesus Christ than I have ever seen. Normally, when I have a conversation to lead someone to the Lord, I expect it to take a lot to convince them. Now, it's like, let's skip all the intro and get down to praying to receive Christ! Last week, I had someone call me and want to get saved. Folks, if you are a believer and walking in the Spirit, you have insight. It's your time to shine like the stars of Heaven. Just follow through with that nudge, believe, and go. He'll take care of the rest.

It Depends Upon How You Look At It

Numbers 13:1 (NKJV) "And the Lord spoke to Moses, saying, ² "Send men to spy out the land of Canaan, which I am giving to the children of Israel; from each tribe of their fathers you shall send a man, every one a leader among them."

The Lord called for men to go in and take a look at the Promised Land that He had promised them. He said to choose one representative from each tribe of Israel. They went in and scoped it out. From the tribe of Judah, Caleb, and from the tribe of Benjamin, Joshua, brought back a report of all the fruit, milk and honey, and wonders of the land God had prepared for those whom He had chosen. All the rest who went with them came back with a report of how big and bad the inhabitants were. (³¹ But the men who had gone up with him said, "We are not able to go up against the people, for they *are* stronger than we.") Even though they brought back a cluster of grapes so big, two men (maybe Joshua and Caleb?) had to carry it on a pole as evidence, and they admitted it was full of riches and wonderful things, they said, we're afraid and we can't pull this off. Of course they weren't able to do it! God said that <u>He</u> would do it. "³⁰ Then Caleb quieted the people before Moses, and said, "Let us go up at once and take possession, for we are well able to overcome it "The ten losers were looking at what they could do and the two victors saw what God told them to look at. The ten died of a plague, the two outlived all their peers and got to go into the Promised Land.

The point here is, from whose perspective are you looking? When God calls us to do something, we have to look at it from His eyes, the eyes of the Holy Spirit. That requires a choice. Am I going to make decisions based upon my old way of thinking or am I going to start seeing what God sees through faith? Mark "2:²² And no one puts new wine into old wineskins; or else the new wine bursts the wineskins, the wine is spilled, and the wineskins are ruined. But new wine must be put into new wineskins." When God puts His "New Wine" (Spirit) in us, when we are born-again, we have to have new "wine skins" to live our new life. We have to see with new eyes. When we do, we will see new things that have been there all along as if we have seen them for the first time. **Colossians 3:1-2** says, "If then you were raised with Christ, seek those things which are above, where Christ is, sitting at the right hand of God. ² Set your mind on things above, not on things on the earth." **Philippians 4:8** says, "Finally, brethren, whatever things are true, whatever things *are* noble, whatever things *are* just, whatever things *are* pure, whatever things *are* lovely, whatever things *are* of good report, if *there is* any virtue and if *there is* anything praiseworthy—meditate on these things."

It's the difference between the guy who says, "Good morning Lord!", or the one who says, "Good Lord! Morning?" As we are surrounded by the world's darkness and wrong things and thinking, we literally have access to the Promised Land which is in us and around us. Look into the Light with the eyes of the Holy Spirit with our prayers, reading His Word, our thinking, our words, and all that we seek this day. All twelve of the Hebrew scouts saw the same things. The ten losers looked at, and believed the wrong things. Joshua and Caleb listened to what God said and chose only to focus on that. That choice is yours to make.

Judgement Free Zone

I've heard the term, "judgement free zone" several times lately. I'm sure the implications can be far ranging, but the truth is, there is only one judgement-free zone. People who claim to be "judgement free" are quick to judge anyone that disagrees with them, saying they are judgmental. The only one who we need to be concerned about judging us is the One who will sit on the Great White Throne on the Day of Judgement. The good news is, that same One who sits on the throne came and hung on a cross to take our place, so if we believe on Him, we will not be judged. He willfully took our judgement for us and became our sin **(2 Corinthians 5:21). 2 Corinthians 5:17** says, "Therefore, if any man be in Christ, He is a new creature. Old things are passed away and all things are made new." The judgement-free zone is IN CHRIST!

Romans 8:1 (NKJV)"There is therefore now no condemnation (judgment) to those who are IN CHRIST JESUS, who do not walk according to the flesh, but according to the Spirit."

Just Believe

Genesis 3:4 (NKJV) "Then the serpent said to the woman, "You will not surely die. ⁵ For God knows that in the day you eat of it your eyes will be opened, and you will be like God, knowing good and evil."
⁶ So when the woman saw that the tree *was* good for food, that it *was* pleasant to the eyes, and a tree desirable to make *one* wise, she took of its fruit and ate. She also gave to her husband with her, and he ate."

Genesis 15:6
"And he (Abraham) believed in the Lord, and He accounted it to him for righteousness."

Romans 10:9
"… if you confess with your mouth the Lord Jesus and believe in your heart that God has raised Him from the dead, you will be saved."

All this mess started the moment Eve and Adam focused on the serpent and took their focus off of the Lord. They listened one moment to the lie, pondered it, began to doubt the Truth, believed the lie, then, they acted upon it which resulted in disobedience. The fall did not begin with disobedience. It began with unbelief. The unbelief began when Satan turned their focus off of the Lord and onto themselves. They were warned what would happen when that took place. Death was invited, their dominion over the earthly realm was handed over to Satan, and the curse began. That's why the world is the way it is today. That is why there is darkness, confusion, sin, selfishness, sickness, sorrow, loss, grief, sadness, and so on, because… the wages of sin is death,

BUT the gift of God is eternal life in Christ Jesus our Lord! (Romans 6:23) Because of God's love (John 3:16…you know it), Jesus, who never sinned, took our place and took the wages of sin. He died for us and made it where we need do the only logical thing to correct where we failed. BELIEVE!

Unbelief disconnected us from God. Now through Jesus, belief reconnects us. **Acts 16:31**

So they said, "Believe on the Lord Jesus Christ, and you will be saved, you and your household." Some verses say repent and believe (makes sense, "sorry for unbelieving, now I believe"), other verses say believe and be baptized (Baptism is my affirmation with and obedience to God and confession to man that I believe), but some verses just say "believe" by itself (like Romans 10:9). Even the thief on the cross (Luke 23:43) whom Jesus told would be with Him that day in Paradise, only had time to ask (because, suddenly believed). Abraham did one thing to obtain righteousness; he believed. It wasn't circumcision; it wasn't baptism; he didn't have to go and do good deeds. He just believed. That resulted in obedience because that's what happens when you believe.

How do I believe? Don't make it complicated or hard. **Matthew 18:3** …"Assuredly, I say to you, unless you are converted and become as little children, you will by no means enter the kingdom of heaven.

Go back to the childlike faith; you know, "Jesus loves me this I know, for the Bible tells me so" faith. Go with Jesus, back to where Adam and Eve were in the garden, before they blew it. Be sorry for your sins, believe that Jesus gave His life to take your place and that He rose from the dead. Believe and He will come inside of you and give you that life back that the unbelief took away. Then, obey, be baptized, worship, commune, serve, and grow closer to Jesus. Believing, though, is what gets you back in.

Just Scratching the Surface

Daniel 9:3 (NKJV) "Then I set my face toward the Lord God to make request by prayer and supplications, with fasting, sackcloth, and ashes. ⁴ And I prayed to the LORD my God, and made confession…"

Do you ever feel like you have gotten to a place spiritually where you get stuck and you just can't move forward? Some people believe that there is just no more to learn and no farther to go. Others think God has deserted them and others begin to question if any of it was true after all. Whatever the outcome is, the worst thing one can do is to quit seeking. It is like getting stuck in the mud or snow and just cutting the engine off and giving up to freeze to death.

I recently did another read-straight-through-the Bible time, reading fast enough to make decent progress each day, yet slow enough to try to see new things I missed other times. I believe that you can read the same verse every day and get more out of it because the Bible is the Living Word and connects with the Holy Spirit inside of you, speaking directly to you and your life. From the creation, to the measurements of the tabernacle, to the laws, miracles, direct messages from God, character and actions of the people, prophecies, etc., I saw new things, new revelations, light, and life that I had not seen before.

For the last few days, I have felt bogged down and stuck again. I was not feeling the intimacy during prayer time, nor the fresh revelation from the Word. Even though I read it every day, I was getting distracted and having to go back and read the paragraph I had just read. I was even feeling like prayers weren't being heard, wondering if I was out of sorts with God. Then, a couple of days ago, I felt like I was supposed to go back through the book of Daniel. If you think you think you will ever run out of insight and revelation, read chapters 9 and 10. Angels appear to him in full glory, enough to knock him down and he had to be touched more than once to give him strength to even stand up. Then he was given prophecies that were so detailed and powerful, it could take centuries to understand them. And this was not a one-time occurrence! He got to know this regular visitor by name; Gabriel.

Here's what I noticed about Daniel. He prayed regularly to God, no matter what the circumstances or obstacles were. When he really needed an answer, he would stay in the presence of God until he got it (like when Nebuchadnezzar was going to kill them if they didn't have the interpretation). He would often fast in sackcloth and ashes, even if it took three weeks. It blows my mind when I think about the spiritual battle that took Gabriel three weeks to get to Daniel! (What does that even look like?) When I see the depth of all that, and that even Daniel was just seeing the "trailers" of the "real movie", I realize that I have just scratched the surface. Keep digging. Keep praying. Keep reading the Word. You might have a little dry spell, but don't stop there. There is exceedingly, abundantly, much more. (**Eph. 3:20**).

Last Night's Dream, Jesus Came Back

Last night, I dreamed that Jesus came back, in fact, this is still "last night" because I got up to write it before I forgot any of it. Miraculously, I am sitting here typing without my glasses, because I forgot them and I don't even want to get up and get them so I don't lose my train of thought. This is not a dream about the Rapture (I had one of those about 40+ years ago). This is about the literal Second Coming of Christ.

All I can tell you is, we were in our immortal bodies. We couldn't be killed, and we had nothing to fear, ever, again. Jesus had just gotten here and was taking charge in His rule of the earth. In this dream, I remember being able to communicate with people who were hundreds of miles away without a phone or anything electronic. We would just set our minds on the Heavenly realm and it was like we would rise up above where we were, even our time we were in, and communicate. We were the Saints, who were already working with Jesus and we were establishing everything and putting everything and everyone in order under Jesus' reign. The wonderful thing was, just as you would imagine, Jesus was right there in the mix of things, walking around with His people. He wasn't in some distant office or on a throne far away. He was walking right there among us. Even though He was in the midst of it all, when I walked by Him, He looked at me and smiled and came up and hugged me, as I did Him, and we held each other, and I wept. Right then, I was included in the work that was being done and I was a part of it all. Then I woke up.

Leaven

Luke 12:1 (NKJV) "In the meantime, when an innumerable multitude of people had gathered together, so that they trampled one another, He began to say to His disciples first of all, "Beware of the leaven of the Pharisees, which is hypocrisy."

Six different times in the New Testament, Jesus warns the people to "beware the leaven" of the Pharisees. In Revelation, He tells the people how the doctrines and deeds of the Nicolaitans (of which I have written a book about) and the teachings of Balaam have come into certain churches of Asia as well as the false teachings and despicable acts of Jezebel. In Scripture, leaven is often equated with sin. The Israelites celebrated Passover with unleavened bread because God told them to make it that way. That's why I would rather take communion with unleavened bread. When you make bread, you take the same flour, water, salt, etc. and add an unnoticeable bit of yeast, starter, or some type of leaven to alter the entire appearance of the substance. When it is first added, you don't notice a difference. After it is there for a period of time, it has altered the entire loaf into something totally different.

I was watching protesters on college campuses, literally persecuting Jews (Sound familiar? I wonder who is inspiring that?). I wondered how so many college aged students could be swayed to see right as wrong, dark as light, etc., and be so clueless as to the truth. I was reading an article in Jim Denison's "Daily News" this morning and noticed that there were professors instigating and fueling these protests. One Columbia University professor was praising the attacks on the Jewish students while another said that every ugly, despicable, pernicious act on the earth could be traced back to the Jews. Then I realized it was leaven.

Leaven is a fungus based thing. It can be good or bad, but the devil likes to use it for bad and it is his most effective weapon. That is why so many people who identify themselves as "Christian" today think it is normal to doubt the Bible and the basic beliefs that it teaches. When I was a freshman in college, I was in a class full of 18 year old kids who had just left home and the Old and New Testament professors began to insert that leaven. They told us to forget what our parents and grandparents taught us and decide for ourselves. That sounded great to a lot of the students. Then they started to tell us that the Bible wasn't really inspired by God, or if so, it was altered by man and written full of errors at best. Many of us did not buy what they were selling because we knew the One who wrote it. We had already experienced how the Bible came alive to us after we were born-again and received the Spirit of God within us. I saw others, though, slowly transformed into another person right before my eyes. I also noticed that virtually all of them were ok with sin, because they were taught that there really was no such thing. Many fell into blatant sinful lifestyles and others were more subtle. They would get into a pulpit and have the appearance of a gifted representative of God, but they would begin to sow the same leaven into the congregation. That tactic has resulted in what we see today with the "great falling away" in the Church.

The good news is, Romans 5:20 says where sin abounds, grace much more abounds. In other words, God is a lot mightier than the devil. Revival is happening now all over the world. People are coming to Jesus! Just like His Word said in Acts 2 and Joel 2. Let's keep spreading the seed of the Word of God, not the leaven of unbelief! Amen!

Living In the Rock

Psalms 18:1 (NKJV) "I will love You, O LORD, my strength.
² The LORD is my rock and my fortress and my deliverer;
My God, my strength, in whom I will trust;
My shield and the horn of my salvation, my stronghold.
³ I will call upon the LORD, *who is worthy* to be praised;
So shall I be saved from my enemies."

I was singing the song this morning,
"Praise the name of Jesus, Praise the name of Jesus
He's my rock, He's my Fortress, He's my deliverer
In Him will I trust, Praise the name of Jesus".

When I sang it, I saw myself standing in a giant rock like a fortress. Then I saw Jesus delivering me from my enemies. When we put our trust in Jesus, we are standing on a solid Rock, we are surrounded and covered by this Rock which is impenetrable. **Psalm 91** says something similar. Verses 1 and 2 say,

"He who dwells in the secret place of the Most High
Shall abide under the shadow of the Almighty.
² I will say of the Lord, "*He is* my refuge and my fortress;
My God, in Him I will trust." (read the whole chapter, in fact, memorize it).

The secret to standing and not falling, to falling and getting back up, to overcoming the enemy, to staying faithful, is to stay in that place of being IN Jesus. Not thinking about Him, doing a good deed, not philosophizing or doing something that looks religious, but yielding, surrendering, submitting, WANTING Jesus to encompass you and your life. **Ephesians 1:3** says,

"Blessed be the God and Father of our Lord Jesus Christ, who has blessed us with every spiritual blessing in the heavenly places in Christ."

When we read this, we get excited about being "blessed with every spiritual blessing", but I get even more excited about being in "the heavenly places", not just with, but "IN Christ"! Verse 9 refers to us having made known the "mystery of His will" that He may gather to Himself all things "IN CHRIST". That is the mystery that the whole universe has been waiting to be revealed. Through the death and resurrection of Jesus Christ, we who believe are now resurrected with Him and are literally IN HIM! So now 2 Corinthians 5:17 is clear, "Therefore if any man be IN CHRIST, he is a new creation. Old things are passed away and all things are made new".

As we find ourselves living in this time that seems out of control, remember, the Creator knows the outcome and we are on the winning side. Do not focus on the world and the insane things that are going on. Stand and live in the Rock, the Fortress, and the Deliverer.

Look Around You

---

2 Peter 3:3 (ESV) "Knowing this first of all, that scoffers will come in the last days with scoffing, following their own sinful desires. 4 They will say, "Where is the promise of his coming? For ever since the fathers fell asleep, all things are continuing as they were from the beginning of creation."
¹¹ Therefore, since all these things will be dissolved, what manner *of persons* ought you to be in holy conduct and godliness, ¹² looking for and hastening the coming of the day of God, because of which the heavens will be dissolved, being on fire, and the elements will melt with fervent heat? ¹³ Nevertheless we, according to His promise, look for new heavens and a new earth in which righteousness dwells."

All the time, and just recently, I've heard people say, "Paul and the other apostles were looking for the coming of Jesus and it didn't happen; people throughout the ages said the same thing and it didn't happen. It probably won't happen during our lifetime." Peter said the normal posture for a believer should be looking up. "Looking for and hastening the day…" Peter and Paul were not wrong in looking for it. Peter said it would keep us in lives of holiness and godliness. Even if it doesn't happen during our lifetime, that last word should get your attention; lifetime. It's the same result. If Jesus doesn't come back while you are alive, you will still cease to remain on this earth. You will still have to give account. You still need to be ready.

Another thing they misquote is that Jesus said no one would know when that time is. Quite the opposite. They take the verse, **Matthew 24: 36** "But concerning that day and hour no one knows, not even the angels of heaven, nor the Son, but the Father only…" He said, "day and hour". Beginning in verse 32, He said, "32 "From the fig tree learn its lesson: as soon as its branch becomes tender and puts out its leaves, you know that summer is near. 33 So also, when you see all these things, you know that he is near, at the very gates. 34 Truly, I say to you, this generation will not pass away until all these things take place." This generation is the one who sees everything falling into place at once or the "fig tree budding." So, we don't know the day nor the hour, but He tells us to know the generation.

My question is this, how can you look at what's going on around you and say nothing is happening? If there were no Bible prophecies at all, plain common sense would tell you that we are about to end it ourselves in multiple ways. Wars, pollution, overpopulation, disease, climate change, AI, crime, mass shootings, terrorists, hatred, natural disasters, etc., are threatening us on multiple fronts. Our "blessed hope" is that Jesus is coming back to reign and make things right before we take ourselves completely out.

Bottom line is this: can you be both a "scoffer" (**2 Peter 3:3**) and a follower of Jesus Christ who is living in holiness and godliness (verses 11-12)? Psalm 1:1 Blessed is the man who walks not in the counsel of the wicked, nor stands in the way of sinners, nor sits in the seat of scoffers; ² but his delight is in the law of the Lord, and on his law he meditates day and night ("waiting for and hastening").

It's Looking More Like
What It Will Look Like

Malachi 3:16 (NKJV)
"Then those who feared the LORD spoke to one another, And the LORD listened and heard *them;*
So a book of remembrance was written before Him
For those who fear the LORD
And who meditate on His name.
¹⁷ "They shall be Mine," says the LORD of hosts,
"On the day that I make them My jewels. And I will spare them
As a man spares his own son who serves him."
¹⁸ Then you shall again discern between the righteous and the wicked,
Between one who serves God and one who does not serve Him."

When the Lord returns, this is a picture of what life will look like. Love, joy, fellowship. It says we will be made His "jewels". That sounds just like **1 Peter 2:9**, "But you are a chosen generation, a royal priesthood, a holy nation, His own special people, that you may proclaim the praises of Him who called you out of darkness into His marvelous light;".

This can also be used to describe God's people today who are waiting for the glorious appearing of Jesus Christ. The closer we get, the more wicked the world gets, but the more God's people have their eyes on Him, thus, walking in holiness. Verse 18 says that "you will again discern between the righteous and the wicked, between the one who serves God and the one who does not serve Him." I've noticed on shows and movies in the last few years, the main characters do worse things than the "bad guys" did a few years ago. Yet they are supposed to be the "protagonists". I just saw a commercial where a kid's show was made up of "heroes" who were "villians". That is satan's not-so-subtle way of making evil the norm. The church has done it too. Trying to make Christians look like the world where you can't tell the difference. However, I've seen an uptick in God's people living the Christian walk and letting their light shine lately. You can tell the difference more today. The only catch to it is, when we do, we need to expect the world to hate it. When we turn on the light, it exposes the darkness. **2 Timothy 3:12** confirms that when it says, "Yes, and all who desire to live godly in Christ Jesus will suffer persecution." I am convinced though, that God's greatest blessings and anointing comes during that time. The dividing line is wider and more distinguishable and will continue to be that way until the final confrontation between dark and Light and the darkness is cast out. That is the full manifestation of Malachi 3:16-17. It is also described in almost all the prophets in the Bible in one way or another.

Revelation 22:10-12 sums it up, "And he said to me, "Do not seal up the words of the prophecy of this book, for the time is near. 11 Let the evildoer still do evil, and the filthy still be filthy, and the righteous still do right, and the holy still be holy."12 "Behold, I am coming soon, bringing my recompense with me, to repay each one for what he has done. 13 I am the Alpha and the Omega, the first and the last, the beginning and the end."14 Blessed are those who wash their robes, so that they may have the right to the tree of life and that they may enter the city by the gates.

Love = Obey

John 14:15 (NKJV) "If you love Me, keep My commandments. [16] And I will pray the Father, and He will give you another Helper, that He may abide with you forever— [17] the Spirit of truth, whom the world cannot receive, because it neither sees Him nor knows Him; but you know Him, for He dwells with you and will be in you. [18] I will not leave you orphans; I will come to you.

[21] He who has My commandments and keeps them, it is he who loves Me. And he who loves Me will be loved by My Father, and I will love him and manifest Myself to him."

Many parents are duped into believing that if they love their child, they must give them whatever they want. When they do this, they are teaching them the opposite of the nature of God. Jesus, quoting the Scripture, said to love the Lord with all your heart, soul, and strength (**Deut. 6:5**), and to love your neighbor as yourself (**Luke 10:27**). I call this the "Divine Order". 1-Love the Lord, 2-love your neighbor, 3-as yourself (He didn't even have to tell you to love yourself). We live in a world that flows against that principle. I call that "The Natural Order". When we meet Jesus and are born-again, He transforms our old self that follows the natural order into a new self that learns to follow the divine order. God becomes the priority. Jesus said in Matthew 6:33, if we seek the kingdom of God first, all the rest will be taken care of. We can quit worrying about our self and let Him take care of that for us. We fall in love with Jesus when we meet Him, and we change our perspective from having to keep His commandments into wanting to.

Even after our salvation experience, our human nature, flesh, selfish state of mind, etc., wants to fight against God's order of things. We want to go to Heaven, to serve God, to be a better person, overcome old sins and habits, but we still want to be in charge. Our spirit has already connected with God after being born again, and wants to be in that fellowship with Him, but our flesh fights against the spirit. Paul talked about his battle with it in **Romans 7:21-25**. We would lose that battle without some help. But Jesus said that He was sending us a Helper. The Holy Spirit. He came in and joined with our spirit when we gave our life to Christ. Now we have God Himself helping us to win over the flesh. We now have the power to obey Him.

So, here it is: Jesus said loving Him and keeping His commandments were inseparable. You can't have one without the other. But then He said, I will give you the ability to do that. I will send my Spirit to help you; basically, do it through you. When you mess up, I have a reset button called repentance that you can use until you get home. And best of all, I have already made you perfect in the eyes of My Father. When He sees you, He sees Me, because I took your place and you are now in Me. Want to stay out of trouble? Walk as close to Me as possible. That's where I want you anyway because I love you!

If You Love Him, You Want To Keep His Commandments

John 14:15 (NKJV) "If you love Me, keep My commandments. 16 And I will pray the Father, and He will give you another Helper, that He may abide with you forever— 17 the Spirit of truth, whom the world cannot receive, because it neither sees Him nor knows Him; but you know Him, for He dwells with you and will be in you."

In these verses, Jesus first says to keep His commandments if we love Him. Immediately after that He says that He will pray for the Father to send us a Helper.

When I first became a born-again believer, something immediately changed. God Himself came inside of me and transformed me. I fell in love with the source of Love. I wanted to do His will and I wanted to obey His commandments. I would like to say that I quit sinning, but I didn't even make it through that day without sin. But what did happen was, my "want-to's" changed. It's kind of like when someone falls in love. The old things that you used to cling to, the things that made you happy, all of a sudden changed. The new person in your life has your focus and the things that they like, all of a sudden you like. One of my mentors when I was a young Christian told me that he used to love to go quail hunting whenever he had any spare time. After he met Jesus, he wasn't interested in quail hunting much anymore. He said that it was not a sin to quail hunt, it was just that Jesus gave him much more and better things for him to want to do. He said God changed his "want-to's".

That love, empowered by the Holy Spirit inside of me transformed my spirit immediately and started transforming my thinking and actions at that point. Some of my old bad habits and sins changed very quickly and others, I am still working on. But the Living Savior lives in me now and helps me by giving me that constant companionship, reminding me, convicting me, patching me up, picking me up and putting me back on my feet. That is how this Christianity thing works. It's alive, He's alive, and He made me alive.

Do you want to keep His commandments? It's because you love Him. Having trouble keeping them? He will help you if He lives inside of you because He loves you.

Love Your Enemies

Matthew 5:43-48 (NKJV) "You have heard that it was said, 'You shall love your neighbor and hate your enemy.' But I say to you, love your enemies, bless those who curse you, do good to those who hate you, and pray for those who spitefully use you and persecute you, that you may be sons of your Father in heaven; for He makes His sun rise on the evil and on the good, and sends rain on the just and on the unjust. ..."

There will be nothing but love in God's kingdom. There is nothing but love there now. If you are not walking and living in love, you are not dwelling in His kingdom. There is someone in every Christian's life who is a challenge, a person who is hard to love, someone who you absolutely hate, or, more commonly, someone who just doesn't matter either way (whoops, I believe that one gets all of our "toes"). When James and John asked Jesus to call down fire on the Samaritan village that did not receive them, He said, "You do not know what manner of spirit you are of. For the Son of Man did not come to destroy men's lives but to save them."(**Luke 9:51-56**). We have those people in our lives whom we shove out of our minds, but we have not truly forgiven them. Just to be blunt, we cringe when we see them. We still do not love them. I was thinking recently, would I be comfortable, seeing them in Heaven? Even worse, would I be comfortable, NOT seeing them in Heaven?!! Maybe I am the one who would not be seen in Heaven! (**Matthew 7:21-23**).

Want me to lighten up? I am sending an urgent warning to the Body of Christ that among all the important things that we need to be doing today, repentance, faith, helping, witnessing, holiness, miracles; faith, hope, love; the greatest of these is LOVE! (**1 Cor. 13:13**). I hate what Hamas did to the Israelis. I hate what the Russians did to the Ukrainians. I hate all the shooting, lying, selfishness, and evil that is going on the world. But the way to fix it is to let God fix it through us and GOD IS LOVE! You want to "fix" your enemy? LOVE THEM! You admit that you can't do it? Now we are getting somewhere! Surrender your thoughts, emotions, "rights", and yourself to God. Let them be crucified on the cross and buried under the water, and ask God to do it through you. You might or might not feel it at first, but keep putting it there. God will help you. **Matthew 19:26** says, "But Jesus looked at them and said to them, "With men this is impossible, but with God all things are possible." Yes Jesus is asking; no, telling, us to love our enemies. That is humanly impossible. Faith and obedience are possible. As we obey, He will release the love of His kingdom and it will flow through us. It is released by obeying God and forgiving. Instead of expecting our enemy to be removed because they make us uncomfortable, expect God to transform them into a new creation just like He did for us. That will change both them and us. In God's perfect will, you will see your enemies in Heaven, but they will be your friends. We entered the Kingdom of Heaven when we were born again, so that needs to start now. Glory to God.

Love, Love, Love

1 Corinthians 13:13 (NKJV) "And now abide faith, hope, love, these three; but the greatest of these is love."

I met with a dear old friend yesterday who is in Hospice care. He had a dream where he saw Jesus and told us things that he could not have known unless Jesus had revealed them to him. I won't go into much detail right now, but two things were emphasized more than any other. One was that the evil in the world goes much deeper than people realize with people who literally hate Jesus. The other is, Jesus has called His people to LOVE, LOVE, LOVE. We do not have time to entertain anything that is not love. Starting with each other, and then to the world. We are bombarded and surrounded with sin, hate, unbelief, and darkness. We are to boldly let God's light shine through us with His love. Remember, God is Love (Eph. 4:8).

New Creation

2 Corinthians 5:17 (NKJV) "Therefore, if anyone is in Christ, he is a new creation; old things have passed away; behold, all things have become new."

The beautiful butterfly used to be a completely different creature. It crawled on the ground, foraged for food, always had its head down, looking at the ground. Then it came time for something to change and it attached itself to a limb or structure that was higher than where it used to be. Rather than spinning a silk cocoon like a moth, the butterfly caterpillar was encased by an exoskeleton called a chrysalis that formed around it. Then something miraculous happened. There was a transformation that took place that only the Creator could do. This caterpillar was remade into a beautiful, glorious, creature that spread its wings and soars around showing God's glory and beauty. I glides and floats on the wind and eats nectar from flowers.

This is an expression of God's divine artistry, but even greater, an expression of His love and redemption. When we are born-again, like the butterfly, we are changed into what God created us to be. We can fly, glide, soar, and ride on the wings of His Holy Wind. We can spread our wings wide where people can witness God's beauty. We can drink His living water and eat the nectar of His Word. We are no longer living just to eat and survive, but we are living the life God intended for us with a purpose.

The only thing the caterpillar could do for this to take place was to attach its self to something that was higher. We can attach to Someone higher by faith. We surrender the old us and believe by attaching to the Vine. He covers us with His wings and remakes us into our new selves. Here's the question: are you a "new you" or has your life changed? You cannot change yourself into a new creation any more than a caterpillar can change itself into a butterfly. God has to do it. Many go through life and think they are Christians because they believe certain doctrines, say certain words, and do certain deeds, but they still look like caterpillars. Let go of the old life, believe and attach yourself to Jesus, and be reborn into a new creation.

No Doubt

James 1:5-7 (NKJV)" If any of you lacks wisdom, let him ask of God, who gives to all liberally and without reproach, and it will be given to him. ⁶ But let him ask in faith, with no doubting, for he who doubts is like a wave of the sea driven and tossed by the wind. ⁷ For let not that man suppose that he will receive anything from the Lord;"

Matthew 21:21 "So Jesus answered and said to them, "Assuredly, I say to you, if you have faith and do not doubt, you will not only do what was done to the fig tree, but also if you say to this mountain, 'Be removed and be cast into the sea,' it will be done."

When I was 18 years old and a freshman in college, I had an Old Testament professor tell us that it was his job to "tear down our faith" and cause us to doubt so we could build our own faith based upon our reasoning. He went on to say that we were to forget what our parents and grandparents told us and start all over again. The hidden implication was that we were to believe everything that he told us. By the end of the school year, I saw several completely deny their faith that they grew up with. There was a group of us who were not going to go along with that, and yes, our faith did get stronger because we decided to dig in the Word of God and get grounded in it. For those who quit believing though, it was tragic. One sweet, beautiful, naïve girl who grew up in a small town had completely changed and was living in the boys frat house and using drugs by the end of the year. I still remember her saying, "I used to believe in the Bible and miracles and all those things, but now I don't". This was not just one professor who was teaching that way. It was the majority of them and as I went to other colleges, they were doing the same thing. There was an indoctrination of young, unsuspecting students to doubt God's Word. Now it has spread into every denomination and non-denomination in various degrees. It started with churches watering down the Gospel until it was weak and diluted, then getting away with denying the validity of the Bible, now completely denying God's Word and defiantly condoning abominations that are sending people to hell. How did we get there? By Satan using a non-Biblical means of educating our future leaders who are still young and gullible enough to believe that a man with the man-made title "doctor" knows more than God. They teach us to doubt and not believe. Jesus and James and all the other Holy Spirit enabled writers of the Bible teach us to believe and not doubt.

At the beginning, in the garden, Satan told Adam and Eve to doubt God's Word. All the atrocities that are in the world now started there. It is impossible to please God without faith (**Hebrews 11:6**). **Romans 14:23** says anything not from faith is sin. You will believe something. The question is who will you believe; the one who says to believe God or the other guy? I became a believer 52 years ago and it just keeps getting better.

"Normal" Church

Acts 2:40 (NKJV) "And with many other words he testified and exhorted them, saying, "Be saved from this perverse generation." [41] Then those who gladly received his word were baptized; and that day about three thousand souls were added *to them.* [42] And they continued steadfastly in the apostles' doctrine and fellowship, in the breaking of bread, and in prayers. [43] Then fear came upon every soul, and many wonders and signs were done through the apostles. [44] Now all who believed were together, and had all things in common, [45] and sold their possessions and goods, and divided them among all, as anyone had need.[46] So continuing daily with one accord in the temple, and breaking bread from house to house, they ate their food with gladness and simplicity of heart, [47] praising God and having favor with all the people. And the Lord added to the church daily those who were being saved."

Have you wondered why churches are changing everywhere? Because God is bringing people back to what the early church experienced. Just being real and full of Jesus. When I first got saved, I had a freeing, loving, joyful experience that became a full-time relationship with Jesus. He was no longer some religious figure in my mind that lived far off somewhere; He lived inside of me. Doing traditional, religious, "stuff" at church was not enough. It didn't reflect who He was, because I didn't go to worship a historical, mental image or feeling. I wanted to worship the living God and release Him through my praise and testimony to share with others! Yes, the people at church thought I was weird. Some whispered, "he got religion, but he'll settle down after while". The truth is, the traditions made by man, the pews, the decorations, the stained glass, even the ritual or hymns, none of that brought me that sense of peace or faith anymore. It was the living Savior within me. That's what happened in the early Church.

When the Church began, in **Acts 2**, they gladly received the Word, were saved and baptized. They started listening to and learning the Word, praying, and fellowshipping with each other. Material things became things that they shared with each other because they loved each other so much. They broke bread in the temple (church building), at home, and in each other's homes. They did it with gladness and simplicity of heart, always praising God. They were loving the Lord, their God with all their hearts, minds, souls, and strength, loving their neighbors as themselves. They were not an elite group, a closed group, or a group of people on a higher spiritual plane. They were just real, everyday people who had God's Spirit inside of them, waking them up and remaking them. I noticed how they met, both in the temple, and everywhere else. When they got set free, they quit loving the things in the building and started loving God and each other.

This "phenomenon" that we see today of people dropping labels, manmade rituals and traditions, and stuff in a building, is simply people seeing what it is all about. I see people coming to Jesus on a regular basis. All the old manmade church tradition means nothing to them. They don't get it because many of them didn't grow up in church. They just want to do like the early Church. They want to share the Jesus in them with the Jesus in each other, learn His Word, and simply love. I am convinced that this is the Harvest that Jesus said would happen. We need to be willing to change and flow with it. One last thought: you can read throughout the whole New Testament, and (contrary to what some believe) there are no denominations mentioned. Just this group of joyful and loving people they nicknamed "the Way", later called "Christians". And they just keep spreading.

Not Troubled?

Matthew 24:4 (NKJV) "And Jesus answered and said to them: "Take heed that no one deceives you. ⁵ For many will come in My name, saying, 'I am the Christ,' and will deceive many. ⁶ And you will hear of wars and rumors of wars. **See that you are not troubled**; for all *these things* must come to pass, but the end is not yet. ⁷ For nation will rise against nation, and kingdom against kingdom. And there will be famines, pestilences, and earthquakes in various places. ⁸ All these *are* the beginning of sorrows."

We have watched the recent wars and rumors of wars in the middle east escalating, as well as the Ukraine-Russia conflict, threats from China, North Korea and the news is definitely troubliing. But I go back and read where Jesus said when we see all these things, "see that you are not troubled". How can I not be troubled? Look at what He said, "…for all these things must come to pass, but the end is not yet." Many things are inevitably going to happen that we didn't think would happen that way, but we are not to focus on that. We are to focus on the Kingdom of God. We can look at what will happen after the end, on the other side. We can think about what our lives will be like in Heaven, or helping to rule and reign during the thousand years when Jesus is King on the earth. But we need to be focusing on something more useful for now. We need to focus on sharing the Kingdom of God to the world that is not ready. We need to pray for them, live our testimony in front of them, let God's Spirit flow through us to them, and tell them about Jesus with all the love that we can. I see people coming to Jesus today that have literally surprised me. They are giving themselves in baptism to submit to the Lord and follow Him all their lives. I firmly believe that we are seeing the great outpouring of the Holy Spirit spoken of in Acts chapter 2 and Joel 2. That is what we need to be focusing on! Even if this isn't the time when Christ is about to return, every soul is going to still have to give an account to Jesus when they die. They still need to hear the Gospel. You and I have been commissioned to be the ones to take it to them. If you are going to be troubled, be troubled that there are still people who do not know Jesus and might not live another day. When you do, God will wrap Himself around you, your thoughts, your lives, and you won't be troubled any more.

Nothing But Jesus

Deuteronomy 6:5 (NKJV) "You shall love the Lord your God with all your heart, with all your soul, and with all your strength."

Luke 10:27 So he answered and said, " 'You shall love the Lord your God with all your heart, with all your soul, with all your strength, and with all your mind,' and 'your neighbor as yourself.'"

This morning, I was walking outside and praying. I had that little feeling that something was "off kilter" or out of balance. The song "In Christ Alone" by Keith and Kristen Getty was going on in my head. I started thinking and praying about what it is to serve Jesus only, all the time, with nothing distracting. I'm not just talking about the normal distractions like daily duties, cares of the world, time wasters, or obsessions. I'm talking about times we think we are serving Jesus doing "religious" or "spiritual" things, or even staying busy working for our church. We can get into routines where we are performing rituals or fulfilling duties, all in the flesh, without depending upon the Holy Spirit, or the Holy Spirit doing them through us. When we do this, I believe we are building on the foundation of "wood, hay, and straw" rather than "gold, silver, and precious stones" described in 1 Corinthians 3:11 "For no other foundation can anyone lay than that which is laid, which is Jesus Christ. 12 Now if anyone builds on this foundation with gold, silver, precious stones, wood, hay, straw, 13 each one's work will become clear; for the Day will declare it, because it will be revealed by fire; and the fire will test each one's work, of what sort it is."

So, how do I make it all Jesus? Make Jesus the center of everything. If you are singing and worshipping, forget about how it sounds, looks, or feels; make Jesus the center of it. If you are working in the nursery or taking communion; make Jesus the center of it. If you are at work on Monday; make Jesus the center of it. If you are talking to a friend, eating lunch, driving down the road, digging a hole, building a castle…. You get it; make Jesus the center of it. You see, if you are a Christian, Jesus lives in you and He is the center of you. He goes with you wherever you are. He is a part of you. Recognize that He is the center of everything in your life. And, don't get so busy, even doing "church stuff" that you become like the Church of Ephesus in Revelation 2. They got so busy doing "church stuff" that they lost their first love. They were doing great works, but drifted away from their reason for doing it. Jesus quit being the center of it. But Jesus gave a simple fix for it. He told them to go back to the place before they fell away and return to Him. The same solution is for us today. Go back to our first love, and let Jesus be the center of us.

One Accord

Proverbs 6:16-19 (ESV)

"¹⁶ These six *things* the LORD hates,
Yes, seven *are* an abomination to Him:
¹⁷ A proud look,
A lying tongue,
Hands that shed innocent blood,
¹⁸ A heart that devises wicked plans,
Feet that are swift in running to evil,
¹⁹ A false witness *who* speaks lies,
And one who sows discord among brethren."

I've heard this preached about and read it many times, but the last half of verse 19 stayed on my mind lately. Verses 17 to the first half of 19 talk about the six things that the Lord hates. The seventh one seems to go to another level of depravity; "and one who sows discord among the brethren." Why would that verse be singled out?

I look at **Acts 2** when they were all in the upper room. When God poured out His Spirit upon them, what were they doing? They were praying and seeking the Lord together, "in one accord" (no Honda jokes allowed here, this is serious!). There were initially, at least 514 people who saw Jesus ascend into Heaven, but only 120 were there when the Holy Spirit was poured out. Those who stayed were diligent to pray and wait upon the Lord (**Acts 1:14**). In **Acts 4:24** says that they all raise their voices in one accord, and in vs. 31, it says the whole place was shaken and they were all filled with the Holy Spirit. "One accord" means no discord. When God's power is manifesting in the level it was about to, it would be like being unclean in the presence of the Ark of the Covenant. I have seen God move in mighty miraculous ways when we were all on one accord, praying and worshiping.

Satan knows he can put a damper on that by dividing people. He will throw out thoughts and attitudes that will divide the Body of Christ to prevent God from moving among us. **2 Corinthians 10:5** says, "casting down arguments and every high thing that exalts itself against the knowledge of God, bringing every thought into captivity to the obedience of Christ". How can we get those thoughts under control? Take "I" and "me" out of the equation and put **Jesus** in there instead. **2 Cor. 10:4** says, "For the weapons of our warfare are not carnal but mighty in God for pulling down strongholds". Worship and praise are some of those weapons. They focus us on Jesus and make us ready to receive God's Word. Then we are seeking His Word and will together in faith, making our prayers like a bunch of little fires combined into one giant bonfire.

When you get ready for church today, when the thoughts or words hit you that don't bring you into the presence of the Lord, take authority over them. Recognize the source. Start worshiping, praying, focusing on Jesus, and encouraging others. It will turn that not-so-great worship service into a powerful one, and you will bless and be blessed. Amen

One Church

1 Corinthians 12:12 (NKJV) "For as the body is one and has many members, but all the members of that one body, being many, are one body, so also is Christ. 13 For by one Spirit we were all baptized into one body—whether Jews or Greeks, whether slaves or free—and have all been made to drink into one Spirit. 14 For in fact the body is not one member but many."

Recently, a friend of mine told me about someone in real need and wanted to know if our church could help them out. That person did not live near our church, but I reached out to her. As I was talking to her, she broke down crying and said that God was showing her that He did love her and was listening to her. She had recently gotten saved. She was having a hard time providing for her children because her husband had abandoned them the previous year. She realized that God was there and heard her prayers. Then she asked where our church was, because, naturally if a church helps out, you should go there…right? I said, we are too far for you to drive, but I know of some churches near you that I would recommend. She was again, blown away.

A few months ago, the Holy Spirit showed me an illustration of His Church as if I was looking at a map of our area. While looking at the map, I "zoomed out" and saw a wider area like I do when I want to see rain or snow coming on the radar. On the map, I saw certain churches glowing red and pulsating as "hot spots" where God was moving. Some of the spots were large and others were small, but they were all instrumental in fulfilling God's strategic plan for this plan that is taking place. Revival doesn't seem to be quite the right word. I think it's bigger than that, but it will involve a lot of spiritual warfare and a lot of people laying their lives on the line for Jesus.

I know of churches where God is working tremendously and the people are all in on what is going on. It is a marvelous feeling (been there several times). But if you can "zoom out" a little, you will see that God is doing something at a lot of other places, all different shapes and sizes, simultaneously. What He is doing is a lot bigger that what we can see. When we recognize that we are all part of Acts 2:16-21 and Joel 2:28-32, that means "His Spirit poured out on ALL flesh", we will all act like we do when we get to Heaven. One Body, One Church, One Lord, One purpose; to glorify Jesus Christ.

So God will get the job done. He'll use a church with 5000 and all the high-tech you can imagine. He'll use the little country church with a handful of people who are hungry for the Lord and listening to Him. He'll use the house fellowship in a land where it's illegal to preach the Gospel, He will use the little hut in the jungle. He will use a group of people from different locations, working together to help someone in need and bring them to Christ. Because the Church is His people, His Bride, His New Jerusalem, and we're citizens of the same country.

Want to come to my Church? It's wherever His people are. Can you imagine what that gathering will look like in Heaven? Let's start now.

One More Lap

Hebrews 12:1 (ESV) "Therefore, since we are surrounded by so great a cloud of witnesses, let us also lay aside every weight, and sin which clings so closely, and let us run with endurance the race that is set before us."

I remember the hot football practices, we would work out, do the grass drills, hitting, tumble drills, push-ups when we messed up, and all the rest. Then after a hard work out, we would end the day running sprints on the field. I would get so tired that each step seemed like it would be my last. My two sons ran track and cross-country, their running was even more strenuous and intense than that.

In this whacked-out, "Bizarro World" that we live in, sometimes it seems like it has extended and expended us to the point where we cannot take another step. Our spiritual feet and legs ache, our second wind has run out and there is no more "spizerinktum" (as my grandpa used to say) left. We might get desperate, want to quit, change things, or throw a fit. Maybe it's the prayers for someone that we love to get right with God, get healed, forgive, change. Maybe it's for a situation to change at work, at home, at school, at church. We entertain questions like, "have I missed God?" "Is there some sin in my life keeping my prayers from being answered?" "Does God not like me anymore?"

Then I remember where Jesus told about the persistent widow in Luke 18 who would not quit until her petition was answered. I remember about them continuing to make laps around Jericho until the walls fell down. I remember Simeon and Anna in Luke 2 waiting their entire life for Jesus to be revealed and the man by the pool of Bethesda waiting 38 years to be healed. He was healed both physically and spiritually because he encountered the real Healer. Then there was the woman with the issue of blood who waited 12 years who also encountered the Healer.

We could go on and on, but, what I'm saying is, run one more lap. Walk with Jesus one more day. Be faithful in serving Him one more time. Pray for that lost person one more night. Keep running the race. Hebrews 11 and 12 tells you that it's worth waiting for.

Peace And Safety

1 Thessalonians 5:1 (NKJV) "But concerning the times and the seasons, brethren, you have no need that I should write to you. ² For you yourselves know perfectly that the day of the Lord so comes as a thief in the night. ³ For when they say, "Peace and safety!" then sudden destruction comes upon them, as labor pains upon a pregnant woman. And they shall not escape. ⁴ But you, brethren, are not in darkness, so that this Day should overtake you as a thief. ⁵ You are all sons of light and sons of the day. We are not of the night nor of darkness. ⁶ Therefore let us not sleep, as others *do,* but let us watch and be sober."

Guys! The world is doing what they've always done throughout history. Our admonishment is to stay in the Light and continue to walk in it and let it be seen. We have the Russians, Chinese, Iranians, North Koreans, etc. chomping at the bit to start a war. New diseases worse than Covid out there. Our own people shooting each other. The only thing that is keeping us safe and secure is God's grace. Just like the Israelites, God would protect those who trusted in Him. There are those who would like to make everyone think they are the majority who respond by mocking God on television, worshipping the devil, telling the Creator that He didn't create or that He did it wrong, and just plain denying Him or rejecting Him. In other words, they are acquiescing to the will of Satan because they have played right into his hands. So, they want to push away from the One who protects and delivers us.

If I wasn't already a citizen of God's kingdom, I would be scared to death. Because I belong there and not here, I am not afraid of death (although I don't look forward to the pain that goes along with it). Since we are "children of the day", let's let that Light shine and overcome the darkness around us. When you walk into a dark room, rather than being overwhelmed by the darkness, just flip the switch. Watch the darkness flee.

Power In Numbers

Matthew 18:19 (NKJV) "Again I say to you that if two of you agree on earth concerning anything that they ask, it will be done for them by My Father in heaven. 20 For where two or three are gathered together in My name, I am there in the midst of them."

Ecclesiastes 4:12 "Though one may be overpowered by another, two can withstand him. And a threefold cord is not quickly broken."

As the old adage goes, "there is power in numbers". That can be good or bad. With social media, or even in a democracy, the thinking is, "if I can get enough people to agree with me, I must be right…", (really what that is saying is, "if enough people agree with me, I'll get my way…" or "I won't feel bad about what I'm doing"). The numbers were on the wrong side before the flood during Noah's time. They were wrong at the tower of Babel. They are wrong now when they side against God's Word.

However, when they are on God's side, we might not have that many "likes" or "votes", but we have the One vote that cannot be overridden. In Ecclesiastes 4:12, it shows where two can withstand one bully, bad guy, bad situation, etc., but that third strand "seals the deal". Especially when that third strand is the Lord. The best example is in a marriage. A husband tries to handle things his way in his own time, the wife does the same and not much will get accomplished. They both come together and they can get things done. The problem is, there is another party who tries to interfere with that, and if the enemy (world, flesh, the devil) sees it is working, they will interfere with anything in their arsenal to separate the couple. When a marriage, friendship, two Christians agreeing in prayer, etc. has the third strand being Jesus, the enemy can't stop it. I was praying about some of those situations that have been stubborn that have been going for a long time with no visible results (notice I said "visible results". I know that every prayer for someone is heard). I thought, "we need to double-team this situation." Like having two linemen making a hole for the running back or two people guarding the one basketball player under the goal, and often, the more the merrier.

Deuteronomy 26: 8 says, "Five of you shall chase a hundred, and a hundred of you shall put ten thousand to flight; your enemies shall fall by the sword before you." If I have something major going on in my life that need's God's intervention, I want as many praying as possible. They don't have to know every detail. Some people are so private that they don't want to be on the "prayer chain", but it is better to chunk the pride (which doesn't need to be there anyway), humble yourself and receive the blessing. I don't really care about "good vibes". I don't need mental "energy". I need angels ministering, the Holy Spirit moving and healing, the Word of God activated, and the devil running in many of these situations. "Good vibes" don't do that. "Effective, fervent prayer" does (James 5:16). So, yes, let's let five people pray and chase "a hundred", or even better, get a hundred praying together and put to flight a couple of battalions of the enemy. Let's pray!

Pride and Humility

Numbers 12:3 (NKJV) "Now the man Moses was very humble, more than all men who were on the face of the earth."

Some translations say "meek" rather than "humble". Either way, it doesn't mean "wimpy". It means to have come to a realization that it's all God and none of you. Moses was in a position, the last forty years of his life, where it was all God, or nothing; no Moses. Another equally important element was that in being in that state, it required constant fellowship with the Lord. Moses talked to God all the time. He knew "I AM" more than anyone else. That is what made Moses the most humble man on earth.

When someone says, "that was a good sermon", or "you did well", my answer is always, "He did all the good parts, I did the rest." I know that sounds like false humility, but it's just a fact. I really believe that. I have had many times when, for a brief moment I would believe them, and have to remember where Jesus brought me from and what I would be without Him.

Proverbs 16:18 says, "Pride goes before destruction, and a haughty spirit before a fall." Most of the time it is misquoted and people say "pride goes before a fall". That is true, but it softens it a little bit. That makes it sound like you can just glibly say, "sorry about that, I'll try harder next time". Wording it correctly, it says, "Pride goes before destruction". If you have been destroyed, you are either permanently gone, or you have to be re-created to even exist! I have witnessed the downfall of many a minister of the Gospel because when someone told them how wonderful they were, they began to believe it. Some think that God cannot make it without them. The "celebrity syndrome" kicks in and they begin to stray away from the Truth because they are no longer depending on Jesus. The Holy Spirit becomes the co-pilot rather than the pilot. The first recorded individual who let that happen was once named Lucifer ("Light Bearer", where the root word for "celebrity", and "star" came from), but it was changed to Satan (Usurper). That's where all the bad stuff began. Ministers of the Gospel, stay away from the mirror. When the word "I" is used on a regular basis, back away, lay on your face, and repent. The truth is, God made it without you before, and you can be replaced (ask Judas).

I have also heard that we need to repent of "false pride". That implies there is some kind of good pride. The Bible only mentions pride by itself. On the other hand, there is "false humility", which is a form of pride. One of the most tragic manifestations of false humility is when someone says that they aren't able to share Jesus with others or do God's work. Romans 12:3 says, "For I say, through the grace given to me, to everyone who is among you, not to think of himself more highly than he ought to think, but to think soberly, as God has dealt to each one a measure of faith." Moses used false humility when he said that he wasn't a good speaker. God said, "Ok, then Aaron can do the talking" (my paraphrase). Then Moses wound up doing all the talking.

Ok, that was kind of tough, but the truth is, we all have a measure of faith. We all have a unique ministry (1 Cor. 5:18). Let's complete it by walking as closely to Jesus as we can, and staying humble.

Pride Goes Before Destruction

Proverbs 16:18 (NKJV) "Pride goes before destruction, And a haughty spirit before a fall."

Several years ago, a young man came to me for counseling and prayer because he was under conviction about sin in his life that he needed to get free from. He was literally consumed by this sin and didn't want to give it up, but he knew that the Bible and his grandmother whom he lived with said it was wrong. He also knew it could have a catastrophic impact on people that he was around on a daily basis. He said that he wanted to repent of his sins, and he knew it was against God's will, but asked if it was alright to ask God why it was wrong. I said that I would pray along with him and ask that very thing. While praying, it hit me that to continue participating in that sin would be to put himself and his feelings above what God said, above what his grandmother taught him, and it would ignore how it would affect many other lives. In other words, it would put what he wanted above everyone and everything else. It was the ultimate expression of selfishness. When I shared that with him, his eyes got big, his mouth fell open, and he stood up and shouted, "YES, YES! THAT'S IT!" "Now I know why!" A couple of years later, he contacted me and said that he was doing well, was married, and had a new baby. God had set him free because he truly repented.

What that young man realized was, the letter in the center of the word, pride, is "I". To focus on that letter, is to spend your life trying to be happy and fulfill your dreams by always putting yourself and your desires first. That is the opposite of God's way. Jesus said to seek His kingdom first and His righteousness and all these things (including happiness) will be added to you (Matthew 6:33). Lucifer had that order of things turned around, wanting all the worship to go toward him. This resulted in his fall which he lured mankind into, becoming its fall. Now to follow that pattern, I, others, and (if you believe in one), God, is the order of Satan's pride. What I call the divine order is in Mark 12:30: "And you shall love the Lord your God with all your heart, with all your soul, with all your mind, and with all your strength.' [31] And the second, like *it, is* this: 'You shall love your neighbor as yourself.' There is no other commandment greater than these." Love God, others, self; in that order. That puts self, last, and in a place where God can bless it. It's called humility. It honors and obeys God, loves and cares for others, and leaves room for God to show His love for you.

Satan has been trying to impose his will on man since man began (good line for a song). I remember slogans like, "do your own thing", "if it feels good, do it", "I'll do it my way", and innumerable other catch-phrases focusing on "I, I, I" and "me, me, me". Even Christianity has been pitched as "what's in it for me?" We find ourselves leaving a church service and saying, "I didn't like the music, or the atmosphere wasn't quite right for me." Worst of all, we are now in a generation and culture where we teach our children that everything is about them. They must be the best, the smartest, the best looking, the most popular. We put them first in line and cushion them from every discomfort. Some grow up liking nothing but chicken nuggets and French fries because we wouldn't make the poor darlings ever try anything that they didn't like. We have called it "self-esteem", but we have taught them pride. "I"…. "me". We complain about this generation, but we created it.

Pride aligns with Satan's personality. Biblical pride is not feeling good because you did a good job. It is putting yourself first and wanting to receive glory. It is wanting to be first, have more "likes" on social media, to be self-absorbed, to have it my way. The young man I described learned the divine order when He gave his life to the Lord that day. God changed him and made him into what He had planned. Let's not celebrate "Pride" and all the things that go along with it. That's Satan's personality. Let's celebrate every day, month, year, our entire lives using God's divine order. Worship and obey Him. Love and serve others. Leave "I" to Him.

Psalm 145:1 "I will extol You, my God, O King; And I will bless Your name forever and ever. ² Every day I will bless You, And I will praise Your name forever and ever.³ Great *is* the LORD, and greatly to be praised; And His greatness *is* unsearchable."

Problem Solved

Ecclesiastes 7:20-22 (NKJV)
"For *there is* not a just man on earth who does good
And does not sin.²¹ Also do not take to heart everything people say, Lest you hear your servant cursing you.
²² For many times, also, your own heart has known that even you have cursed others."

How many times have we been hurt, offended; sometimes even gut-punched and our feet knocked out from under us by something someone said? We might immediately want to pick up our Sword and slice them with **James 3** about taming the tongue. (That sounded really spiritual, didn't it)? Really, we want to punch back with words or something more solid. Another temptation is to run to someone, tell them how you got hurt and how evil that person is. Then you can turn a whole group of people against them if you are successful. If you use social media for the same cause, you can turn a whole army against them; maybe the whole world. (Yeah, this sounds extreme, but I know you've though about it because I have).

I have a better idea. Actually it was God's idea. He gave it more like orders, not a suggestion. He said, "But I say to you who hear: Love your enemies, do good to those who hate you, ²⁸ bless those who curse you, and pray for those who spitefully use you. ²⁹ To him who strikes you on the *one* cheek, offer the other also. And from him who takes away your cloak, do not withhold *your* tunic either. ³⁰ Give to everyone who asks of you. And from him who takes away your goods do not ask *them* back. ³¹ And just as you want men to do to you, you also do to them likewise. (**Luke 6:27-31**) What about this one? (**Matthew 5:39**) "But I tell you not to resist an evil person. But whoever slaps you on your right cheek, turn the other to him also." Many of the people on that mountain who heard Jesus say that might have thought, "Is He crazy?" "Now that's going too far. There's no way I can do that!" Let me tell you a secret; that is the most powerful thing you can do. You have just gotten out of the way and, by faith, released God into the situation! Now He can handle it His way (which is probably not going to be sending fire down from Heaven like James and John wanted to do). God can move in by fixing the problem by fixing the person. God knows what went on at his or her home that morning that has them torn up on the inside.

Here's how you can help. Remove the one thing from the situation that is blocking you from blessing and being blessed. That one thing is the words "I" or "me". Like the tree falling in the forest with nobody there theory, if someone throws a rock or says a harsh word and "I" or "me" is not standing there, there's no one for it to hit. That is what Solomon was talking about in the opening verse. First, you ain't special; not in that sense. You have done it too. Second, **Galatians 2:20** says it like this: "I have been crucified with Christ; it is no longer I who live, but Christ lives in me; and the life which I now live in the flesh I live by faith in the Son of God, who loved me and gave Himself for me." If you are crucified with Christ, "I" and "me" are no longer an issue. Jesus bore all the pain and things that offend upon Himself. He took your place (and the other person who hurt you). Now be risen with Him. Reach out to that waitress who was rude, give them a little extra and tell them that Jesus loves them and you would like to pray with them. Show love to that person who offended you and let Jesus minister to them through you. You may, or may not, see instant results, but Jesus and the anointing of the Holy Spirit will be right there. Problem solved!

Proclaim!

---

1 Chronicles 16:23 (NKJV)
"Sing to the Lord, all the earth; proclaim the good news of His salvation from day to day."

I was at the grocery store one day, and saw a young man that I haven't seen in a while. We have become good friends and enjoy talking every time we see each other. He was at one end of the aisle and I was at the other and there was a lady between us. He shouted out, "Hey Bob, what do you know that's worth telling?" At first, I was going to say something normal or casual like "not much", but it hit me that we needed to proclaim His Word every time we can. I just blurted out, "Jesus is coming soon!" The lady in the middle looked at us like we were weird (she's right), and we approached each other and began talking out loud about salvation, Jesus, people being ready, or not, etc.

The time is getting short (even if it weren't, we are supposed to share Jesus every time we get a chance). Let's take advantage of every opportunity to proclaim His good news. Jesus Christ is Lord, He will save you, ask Him today!

Ready When He Needs You

Matthew 21:18 (NKJV) "Now in the morning, as He returned to the city, He was hungry. 19 And seeing a fig tree by the road, He came to it and found nothing on it but leaves, and said to it, "Let no fruit grow on you ever again." Immediately the fig tree withered away."

Some people might read this verse and say, "poor fig tree". The fact of the matter is, the fig tree was created by the Lord, for the Lord. Here's something that most people don't seem to realize; we were created by the Lord, for the Lord. God loves us, but He did not create us to worship us, He created us to worship Him. He did not create us to serve us, He created us to serve Him. A lot of people get disgruntled at God because things are not going their way. Jesus said, "I AM the way." That is the difference between just believing in Jesus or letting Him be Lord of your life. You say, "what's in it for me?" Well, you get to be close, intimate friends with the King and Creator of the universe, you get to have access to His kingdom, and you get to have eternal life. So, when we get that settled, here is what He needs us to do.

Preach the word! Be ready in season and out of season. Convince, rebuke, exhort, with all longsuffering and teaching (**2 Timothy 4:2**). Jesus was hungry and was about to pick His last fig from a tree that He created (John 1). It wasn't ready. Therefore, it had no more purpose on this earth. There were ten bridesmaids waiting for the Groom and were to be ready at any minute. Five of them quit watching and their lamps ran out of oil when the Groom finally came. The door was shut and I was too late. (**Matthew 25:1-13**). **2 Peter 3:12** says that we should be looking for and hastening the coming of the day of God. I have had instances where I felt the little nudge and I responded by sharing the Gospel with individuals right at that moment. It was at that same moment, the Holy Spirit was dealing with them and they prayed right then to receive Jesus as their Lord and Savior. I have had many more times when I missed the opportunity. God is capable of sending someone else their way, but He wanted me to do it then. Thankfully, I didn't wither like the fig tree, but I sure missed out on a blessing. God knew I was going to fail those times. That was part of the preparation for the next time. That's where His grace and patience are so wonderful. He will help us bear that fruit if we stay connected to the Vine. We stay connected by watching for Him and expecting the Holy Spirit to be present in all aspects of our lives. That is, we realize we were created for Him.

Philippians 2:13 "…for it is God who works in you both to will and to do for His good pleasure."

See That You Are Not Troubled

Matthew 24:2 (NKJV) "And Jesus said to them, "Do you not see all these things? Assuredly, I say to you, not one stone shall be left here upon another, that shall not be thrown down."
³ Now as He sat on the Mount of Olives, the disciples came to Him privately, saying, "Tell us, when will these things be? And what will be the sign of Your coming, and of the end of the age?"
⁴ And Jesus answered and said to them: "Take heed that no one deceives you.
⁵ For many will come in My name, saying, 'I am the Christ,' and will deceive many.
⁶ And you will hear of wars and rumors of wars. See that you are not troubled; for all these things must come to pass, but the end is not yet.
⁷ For nation will rise against nation, and kingdom against kingdom. And there will be famines, pestilences, and earthquakes in various places.
⁸ All these are the beginning of sorrows.

"See That You Are Not Troubled"?! We are living in times that fit exactly with many more Bible prophecies that just this one. How can Jesus say, "See That You Are Not Troubled"? Also phrases like "fear not", "be not anxious", "don't be afraid"? Because when we meet Jesus, if we truly know Him, our citizenship changes and we no longer belong here (**Philippians 3:20** For our citizenship is in heaven, from which we also eagerly wait for the Savior, the Lord Jesus Christ,). When we are reborn, our old self has already died. The enemy has gotten us to a place where we don't want to go a day without AC, internet, TV, fast food, all the conveniences that were once considered luxuries. Many who say they are believers might turn their backs on the faith if they had to go without these things. If we catch ourselves "being troubled", fearing, worrying, (which I do sometimes), we need to immediately focus back on our relationship with Jesus, have that intimate time with the Holy Spirit, and get ourselves back to that place where we long to be with the Father. Then we have put our hearts back into the Kingdom, where we belong. Fear disappears.

Sharing His Spirit-Always His Plan

Numbers 11:16-30 (NKJV) You wouldn't expect to read about a Pentecostal experience in the book of Numbers, but in chapter 11, after the children of Israel complained (again), these 600,000 men, plus their families were a bit overwhelming for Moses. Then Moses cried out to the Lord (summing it up) saying, "I can't do this!!!" The Lord told Moses to round up 70 elders of the tribes of Israel and let them stand there with him at the Tabernacle or Meeting. In verse 17, He said, "Then I will come down and talk with you there. I will take of the Spirit that is upon you and will put the same upon them; and they shall bear the burden of the people with you, that you may not bear it yourself alone." Then, in verse 25, "Then the LORD came down in the cloud, and spoke to him, and took of the Spirit that was upon him, and placed the same upon the seventy elders; and it happened, when the Spirit rested upon them, that they prophesied, although they never did so again. There were two of the elders who never made it to the meeting, Eldad and Medad (I promise, no "Dad" jokes), and a young man came running up and told Moses that there were two prophesying out in the camp. "²⁸ So Joshua the son of Nun, Moses' assistant, one of his choice men, answered and said, "Moses my lord, forbid them!" ²⁹ Then Moses said to him, "Are you zealous for my sake? **Oh, that all the Lord's people were prophets _and_ that the Lord would put His Spirit upon them!**" ³⁰ And Moses returned to the camp, he and the elders of Israel."

There are lots of parallels here! In **Luke 9: 49-50**, we see a similar statement being made by Jesus: "Now John answered and said, "Master, we saw someone casting out demons in Your name, and we forbade him because he does not follow with us. "But Jesus said to him, **"Do not forbid him, for he who is not against us is on our side."** In the beginning of the same chapter, Jesus had equipped the twelve disciples to go out and heal the sick, cast out demons, and preach the Gospel. Here is the closest parallel I noticed: in Luke 10, Jesus sent out... 70! He gave them the same commission as the 12 with the same need that Moses had; the mission was too big for one, or twelve, or even seventy! In Acts 2, on the day of Pentecost, God did it again.

He poured out His Spirit on the 120, they performed signs and wonders, spoke in tongues, prophesied, and the Gospel was spread. The outpouring didn't end then. Three thousand souls came to Christ that day. In Acts 4, there was another outpouring, the ground shook, many were saved and filled with the Holy Spirit and proclaimed the Word of God boldly.

The prophecy in Acts 2, spoken in Joel 2, said "in the last days, I will pour out my Spirit upon all flesh." I believe the "last days" started over 2000 years ago, but I also believe that the prophecy predicts an outpouring at the last of the last days which I think is now. People are getting saved in large numbers, miracles are happening, and God is doing things that have never happened before all over the world. More people are believing on Jesus in countries that forbid the Gospel and persecute Christians than in the "free world". People who have never been taught about Jesus are having miraculous manifestations from Him and following Jesus.

My point is, the Harvest is here. God is pouring out His Spirit and calling and equipping much more than 70! He is calling us to function as the Body of Christ, step out in faith and operate in our gifts and do things that we never imagined that we could do. It has been God's will to share and disperse His Spirit with His people since day-one. There are people sitting out in churches who need to respond, get up, and go out. Be a participator, not a spectator. Let the Holy Spirit change you, fill you, and empower and enable you. Then you will do things you never even dreamed of.

Snake Dream

1 John 5: 17 (ESV) "All wrongdoing is sin, but there is sin that does not lead to death. [18] We know that everyone who has been born of God does not keep on sinning, but he who was born of God protects him, and the evil one does not touch him."

Recently, I had a dream where I was sitting on the floor, relaxing in front of the couch. Many times, when I am sitting on the couch or lying in the bed, my dog, Annie will come and lay with her back against my leg as if she just wants to make sure I am there. In this dream, I felt something similar and looked and there was a blanket against my leg with something under it. I realized that, instead of my dog, there was a snake under the blanket. It was a non-poisonous rat snake like I see around the house in the yard, so it wasn't deadly, nevertheless, it was a snake and it did not belong there. I hesitantly and lazily grabbed the blanket and picked up the snake and took it out to the woods outside and got rid of it. Unlike most dreams, it was still fresh on my mind when I woke up and I could remember all the details. I was going to sluff it off and forget it, but during my prayer time, the Holy Spirit showed me that the snake represented something I needed to deal with in my life. The snake represented sin that I had grown comfortable with because it didn't seem deadly or even serious. It was in the realm of my thoughts, so no one else knew about it (except the Holy Spirit). The blanket represented two things. One was, it wasn't going to be that hard to get rid of it, just grab it with no risk and toss it. The other was, this wasn't a sin that I had to confess it in front of anyone except the Lord. The point was, it was still sin, and like the snake, it didn't need to live in my "house".

Repenting and being free from sin doesn't just include sins that we think are "the worst" or the ones that are visible to others. We also do not repent of sin because we think it makes God sad or ashamed of us. These little, unnoticed areas can cause us to experience a distancing in our walk with the Lord. Sin is a distraction or a hindrance to our relationship with Jesus. God is a holy God. Jesus shed His blood to remove our sin so we can come back to a full fellowship and close relationship to Him. We were created to walk closely to God and have an intimate relationship with Him. He is not saying, "I won't walk with you until you have no more sin". He is saying, "If you walk with me, I will help you get rid of the sin so we can walk even closer". That's what His grace does, it helps us to become more like Him. He does it because He loves us more than we can ever imagine.

Soar

Isaiah 40:31 (NKJV)
"But those who wait on the Lord Shall renew their strength; They shall mount up with wings like eagles, They shall run and not be weary, They shall walk and not faint."

I love to watch the eagles at when we are at our camper on the lake. We have a couple nesting somewhere nearby and it is a treat to see them fishing, foraging, flying, and fooling with the other birds, like when they are showing the local ospreys who is boss. The most majestic and wonderful sight is when you see one catch an updraft and soar up so high that you almost can't see it. It spreads its wings and the longer it holds them out, the higher it goes without any effort except for just waiting.

The Greek word for Spirit is Pneuma, which can also be translated "breath" or "wind". God often puts us in situations where there is no way for us to do anything about it except wait. I've tried to make them happen by figuring out a way, manipulating, thinking outside the box, and there's just no way to make it happen. So, the only thing left to do is wait. I've learned that there are two ways to wait. One is to wait while being anxious, negative; even growing into bitterness or anger, and the other way is to spread out those wings (in my mind and heart, or even lifting my hands and voice) and focus on the wind. Let God's Spirit just lift me higher and higher until I've reached heights that I've never imagined before and during that hourly, daily, yearly, span of time, I have been right where I needed to be, in the presence of the Lord.

Something Impossible for God?

Hebrews 6:18 (ESV) "…so that by two unchangeable things, in which it is impossible for God to lie, we who have fled for refuge might have strong encouragement to hold fast to the hope set before us."

Psalm 138:2
"I will worship toward Your holy temple,
And praise Your name
For Your lovingkindness and Your truth;
For You have magnified Your word above all Your name"

John 14:6 "Jesus said to him, "I am the way, the truth, and the life. No one comes to the Father, except through Me."

God IS Truth! He is what Truth comes from because He is the source of it. Just like God is Love. He doesn't just have a lot of love; He is made out of it. God cannot lie. It is not in Him. The devil is the father of lies and there is no truth in him (John 8:44). The father of lies wants us to believe that God lies. He tried that in the very beginning when he tempted Eve to doubt God's word. He does it now when he convinces people that the Bible isn't true. I read God's living word every day and it literally works truth, life, and light down into my soul and spirit, bringing me closer to Him, restoring, correcting, and redirecting my life on a daily basis. If there's one thing I know for certain, it is that God and His Word are absolute Truth and that Truth is absolutely necessary. As important as it is to exalt God's name: Jesus, He has magnified His Word above His name. Sometimes when we are at church, we have such wonderful worship, exalting the name of Jesus, that I feel like I could go home and will have been filled. But that is just building us up for the next part, His Word. That is what transforms and renews and strengthens me. It is more important to get God's Word every day than it is to eat. If you aren't doing it yet, start today and see what happens. Amen

The Holy Spirit Will Guide You Into All Truth

John 16:13 (NKJV)

"However, when He, the Spirit of truth, has come, He will guide you into all truth; for He will not speak on His own authority, but whatever He hears He will speak; and He will tell you things to come."

Reading the Bible with the intellect alone is not enough. It's like trying to Google something with no internet. You push all the right buttons or say the right things, but there is no connection and no results. To say, "I believe in the Bible" and read it without the guidance of the Holy Spirit always results in error or just not understanding it. 1 Corinthians 2:14 says "But the natural man does not receive the things of the Spirit of God, for they are foolishness to him; nor can he know them, because they are spiritually discerned." The natural man is the mind and the flesh. However, the next two verses say, "15 But he who is spiritual judges all things, yet he himself is rightly judged by no one. 16 For "who has known the mind of the Lord that he may instruct Him?" But we have the mind of Christ."

"He who is spiritual" simply means, the person who has God's Spirit. "The mind of Christ" in the last verse is the Holy Spirit. Once we surrender our lives to Jesus and the Holy Spirit enters us, we are connected to the Cloud, that is, the Kingdom of God! Everything written in the Bible comes to life and we begin to let it come in and transform our life as we read it. Each time we read it, we get more out of it. We can read John 3:16 for the hundredth time and get more out of it each time because it literally comes alive and has the power to transform us into His image, bit by bit. Having a hard time understanding the Bible? Make sure you have invited the Holy Spirit into your life by surrendering to Jesus. Still having a hard time? Ask the Holy Spirit to help you each time you read it. It will be like a light turning on inside of you.

Spirit to spirit

Often, I encounter people who just can't understand the Bible, no matter how many times they read it. They can read or hear the same verse over and over and it never seems to connect. The first thing to check in that situation is, have you invited the Holy Spirit to live inside of you? Have you been born again? If so, the next question is, are you walking in the Spirit? (**Galatians 5:16, Romans 8:1-2**).

1 Corinthians 2:14-15 (NKJV) says, "But the natural man does not receive the things of the Spirit of God, for they are foolishness to him; nor can he know them, because they are spiritually discerned. 15 But he who is spiritual judges all things, yet he himself is rightly judged by no one." The "natural man" just means that our earthly bodies and minds cannot grasp God's Word because it takes the Holy Spirit to "translate" it. He makes it come alive in our spirits. That can only happen when the Holy Spirit lives in union with our spirit. That's what it means when it says, "But he who is spiritual". That's not someone who sits on top of a mountain and wears a long robe. It simply means that the Holy Spirit lives in you.

Romans 8:16 says, "The Spirit Himself bears witness with our spirit that we are children of God,". When the Holy Spirit lives in us, He "bears witness with our spirit". He communicates with us. That's why we can talk to God anytime and anywhere. When we are sinning, it cuts off that communication (your spiritual "internet" disconnects). Repentance re-boots it and you are back in touch again. The first and most important question is, though, does He live in you? **Revelation 3:20** says that Jesus is knocking on the door of your heart, asking you to open it and invite Him in to share life with you. **Romans 10:9** and **Acts 16:31** (among many other places) say if you believe in your heart and confess with your mouth God has raised Jesus from the dead, you will be saved. In **John 14:6**, Jesus said if you ask anything in His name, He would do it so that the Father would be glorified in the Son. ...Believe and Ask. His Spirit will come in.

Jeremiah 31:33

But this is the covenant that I will make with the house of Israel after those days, says the Lord: I will put My law in their minds, and write it on their hearts; and I will be their God, and they shall be My people.

Hebrews 8:10

For this is the covenant that I will make with the house of Israel after those days, says the Lord: I will put My laws in their mind and write them on their hearts; and I will be their God, and they shall be My people.

This is exactly what these last two verses are talking about. You won't need some rabbi, priest, preacher, or scholar to show you what God's will is. God Himself, who lives in you, will show you His will with His Word.

Still, Small, Voice

1 Kings 19:11-12 (NKJV)
"Then He said, "Go out, and stand on the mountain before the Lord." And behold, the Lord passed by, and a great and strong wind tore into the mountains and broke the rocks in pieces before the Lord, but the Lord was not in the wind; and after the wind an earthquake, but the Lord was not in the earthquake; 12 and after the earthquake a fire, but the Lord was not in the fire; and after the fire a still small voice."

Just walking down the street towards the coffee shop this morning. Last day of visiting daughter, her husband and grandkids. Even though there were cars going by, people out on the sidewalks, and hustle and bustle, I was in my quiet prayer zone. All of a sudden, unexpected, there was the still small voice. He didn't say a lot, mostly like a hand on the shoulder, but instantly there was joy, peace, hope, faith, and mostly, love. I thank Jesus for His still, small, voice. How many times have we not heeded it? Yet, I couldn't miss way He spoke today among all the other background noise. The only thing that would have blocked it would have been if I'd said, "nah, that wasn't Him, it was just my imagination." That is called unbelief. Next time you hear that voice in your spirit, do like Eli told Samuel to do. Listen.

Striking Instead of Speaking

Numbers 20:11-12 (NKJV) "Then Moses lifted his hand and struck the rock twice with his rod; and water came out abundantly, and the congregation and their animals drank.
¹² Then the Lord spoke to Moses and Aaron, "Because you did not believe Me, to hallow Me in the eyes of the children of Israel, therefore you shall not bring this assembly into the land."

I have heard several good sermons and lessons concerning this Scripture. All of them had merit and points that could be life-changing, but one caught my attention today that I hadn't thought of. The last time God gave them water from the rock, God told Moses to strike the rock. This time, He told Moses to speak to it. Instead, Moses struck it twice. While I was meditating on this, the question came to my mind, why did Moses strike it rather than speak to it? How is that similar to something we might do today? God's answer to Moses said, "because you did not believe Me..." When we are following Jesus and growing in the Spirit, we need to expect change, even on a daily basis. I have learned to never expect God to do answer a prayer the same way twice. In fact, He never answers a prayer because we prayed it a certain way, therefore causing us to have to use the same words each time. That's where man-made religion begins. We see God work in a wonderful way and think if we can repeat whatever we did when that happened, God will do it again. Whether it's a church service, a revival meeting, a personal encounter where we got blessed, or the time when a prayer was answered miraculously, we have to realize that God is not One to be conjured up by a ritual. He is the Living God. Jesus is alive walking beside us, inside of us, and us in Him. People get stuck in rituals and even denominations because they are afraid to take that next step. We get comfortable with the way we did it last time because, hey, it worked, didn't it? I wonder what would have happened of Moses had spoken to that rock? Maybe all of Israel could have made it into the promised land right then.

I once had a small vision or a vivid thought that someone was floating down a big river, like Huckleberry Finn on the Mississippi on a raft. The farther we floated, the nearer we were to the delta where the river opened up into the ocean (Heaven). Once and a while, the raft would stop and camp out on the shore, rest, refill with supplies. Some would enjoy those rest-stops so much that they would stay there and not go on. That is how denominations begin. That is how we get stuck and stop growing in our spiritual walks. Good things happen, but there is so much more to be seen and experienced if we don't stop.

We are nowhere close to that place of outward perfection, so we need to expect each encounter with Him to be different, but better. Until my body starts glowing and I don't get tired or hungry anymore without any pain, I haven't arrived yet. In fact, even when that happens, I bet we still will keep moving "farther up, and farther in" as C.S. Lewis said in *The Last Battle* in the *Chronicles of Narnia*.

So, why did Moses strike the rock? Cause that's what worked last time. Where did the unbelief come in? When God said do it a different way and Moses was not focused in on God. He was frustrated at the people and focused on the problem. Did God still love Moses? Of course. Did Moses fulfill everything he could have? Nope, but he still got to go to the real Promised Land. Will we accomplish everything we could have? Not most of us, but we still will have accomplished way more than we could have dreamed by continuing to walk with Jesus, being led by the Spirit, bearing fruit every day. The good thing about walking in His grace is, when we do fail, He will redeem it and turn it into something even better if we keep on walking.

Talk To Him Like A Friend

Exodus 33:11 (NKJV) "So the Lord spoke to Moses face to face, as a man speaks to his friend. And he would return to the camp, but his servant Joshua the son of Nun, a young man, did not depart from the tabernacle."

John 15:15 "No longer do I call you servants, for a servant does not know what his master is doing; but I have called you friends, for all things that I heard from My Father I have made known to you".

How do I pray? Talk to Him as someone speaks to a friend. If you know Him, He is your friend. If you know Him, He lives inside of you and knows every thought. He knows the things going on in the unseen, spiritual realm around you. He knows what has happened that you didn't see and He knows what will happen next. He is the King and Creator of the universe, yet He wants to be your friend. He wants to be your Abba, Father where, as His child, we can come running up to Him and sit in His lap while He wipes tears from our eyes or laughs with us or tells us things we need to know. (**Galatians 4:6** "And because you are sons, God has sent forth the Spirit of His Son into your hearts, crying out, "Abba, Father!"). He wants us to talk to Him.

Temples

1 Corinthians 6:19-20 (NKJV)
"Or do you not know that your body is the temple of the Holy Spirit who is in you, whom you have from God, and you are not your own? For you were bought at a price; therefore glorify God in your body and in your spirit, which are God's."

I was reading in **1 Chronicles 17** where King David wanted to build a temple for God. God reminded him that He had dwelt in the tabernacle since Moses time and that He did not want David to build a "house of cedar" for him. However, He did say that his son would build a temple and his lineage would be preserved forever (Mary and Jesus were descendants of David and Solomon). Solomon built a magnificent temple with elaborate and ornate carvings, everything made out of gold, the walls paneled with gold, literally one of the wonders of the world. Then, over time, Solomon and Israel became distracted and then tempted by the world, and let sin into their lives and into the temple. Over the next few generations, all of the ornateness was gone, the temple stripped of its treasures by the enemies and finally destroyed.

When Jesus came, He fulfilled what all the sacrifices and ceremonies of the temple were intended for. He became the ultimate sacrifice, eradicating our sins, and making us holy when we simply repent and believe on Him. We are now the temple of the Holy Spirit. If Christ lives in us, we have the same Spirit in us that was in the temple and the Ark of the Covenant. What man could not do, God did. Man did his best, even with the help of God, to build something to honor Him. It still wasn't sufficient. People still try to please God with religion, but it will never be enough to contain His holiness. They build shrines, cathedrals, use beautiful music, rituals, words, actions, and even help others. But that is not enough. We don't need to appease God and hope we've done enough. We need to believe and receive Him inside of us. He built the Temple and it is us. He made it holy by His love, mercy, and grace. Then, we let His holiness shine from within us out to the world.

That Great Light

In **Acts 9, 22, and 26**, the testimony of Paul meeting Jesus Christ is told three times. Each time, it tells how when Paul encountered Christ, there was a great light, so bright that it blinded Paul and he and the others with him fell to the ground. Paul had to be led to Ananias' house where he laid hands on him and prayed for him. Paul was filled with the Spirit and scales fell off his eyes where he could see. Then he was baptized and the adventures began.

In **Acts 12**, when Peter was thrown in prison, awaiting probable death, the other believers were in constant prayer for him. An angel of the Lord appeared beside him and a great light shown there in the prison. Immediately the chains fell off and Peter was freed. In **Matthew 17**, Jesus went up on the mountain and He, Moses, and Elijah were there together. It said Jesus face shone like the sun and his clothes became as white as the light. When Moses came off the mountain after being in the presence of the Lord, his face shown with a light so bright, he had to wear a veil over it so the people could look at him.

This morning, while I was outside praying, I was thinking about that light. I was thinking about how when we get to Heaven, everything will shine with that glory, including us. At first, I thought of it like being in a dark room, then turning on the lights. In reality, if we were to see it now, we would do like Paul did. We would fall on our face or go blind. That light is marvelous, beautiful, indescribable, yet, in God's kingdom, that brightness is normal. That is what we have to look forward to in Heaven, but God wants us to realize that we don't have to wait to die or get raptured to experience it. It is already here… in us!

Jesus said, "I am the light of the world" (**John 8:12**, and **9:5**). He said, "you are the light of the world" (Matthew 5:14). He goes on to say in **Matthew 5:16 (NKJV)**, "Let your light so shine before men, that they may see your good works and glorify your Father in heaven." **Philippians 2:14** says "Do all things without complaining and disputing, 15 that you may become blameless and harmless, children of God without fault in the midst of a crooked and perverse generation, among whom you shine as lights in the world, 16 holding fast the word of life, so that I may rejoice in the day of Christ that I have not run in vain or labored in vain.

When the Holy Spirit enters us when we are born again, God's kingdom enters us. His light come into us. As we walk with Jesus, grow in our faith, and learn to "tap into" the Kingdom of

God, we learn to let that light shine through us. That is our calling. Now the world is darker than it has been since the days of Noah. We need to let that light shine now. We are that generation. **1 Peter 2:9** But you are a chosen generation, a royal priesthood, a holy nation, His own special people, that you may proclaim the praises of Him who called you out of darkness into His marvelous light;

Daniel 12:3 Those who are wise shall shine
Like the brightness of the firmament,
And those who turn many to righteousness
Like the stars forever and ever.

The Daily Reset

Psalms 23:3 He restores my soul...

Recently, I was talking to someone, and at the same time we were talking, she was fooling with her phone and seemed frustrated. It was jammed up and wouldn't do what it was supposed to do. I am no "techie", but I asked, have you restarted it? The answer was no, so she restarted it and it worked fine. Phones, computers, TVs, and many other things need a reset. Long before that technology was invented, the reset was around it was created for us.

In **Matthew 6:34 (ESV)**, Jesus said, "Therefore do not be anxious about tomorrow, for tomorrow will be anxious for itself. Sufficient for the day is its own trouble." God designed us to take care of today's business today. He set the example. In **Genesis 1**, God would create what was to be created that day, then it would say, "and there was evening and there was morning, the first day", then "the second day" and so on until the seventh when He rested. We have our rest at night, then we start the next day a completely new day. Then our "reset" begins again. (**Lamentations 3:22-23** "Through the Lord's mercies we are not consumed, because His compassions fail not. ²³ They are new every morning; Great *is* Your faithfulness."

This is how we do it. Going back to **Psalms 23**, backing up to verse 1, it says, "The Lord is my shepherd; I shall not want. He makes me lie down in green pastures. He leads me beside still waters.." We need to have that time in the green pastures and by the still waters every morning, restarting the day with a clean slate. All the sin, confusion, guilt, worry, anger, fear, hatred, unforgiveness, selfish ambition, selfishness altogether, erased! All of that can be washed away by getting quiet before God, reading His Word, and praying. You can begin your prayers by praising Him, confessing your sin, telling Him what's on your heart, praying for others, submitting to His will for the day. Use the "Lord's Prayer" for an outline (**Matthew 6:9-13**). I usually begin with talking to God, reading the Bible, then having a walking prayer time outside. We need to be washed with the Living Water (**John 7:38, Rev. 7:17**), and filled with the Holy Spirit. The Holy Spirit will replace that list of bad things we just mentioned with love, joy, peace, gentleness, kindness, goodness, patience, self-control, faith, and everything else that is good. Our mind will be renewed (**Romans 12:2** Do not be conformed to this world, but be transformed by the renewal of your mind, that by testing you may discern what is the will of God, what is good and acceptable and perfect.)

Here's the thing… we need this reset every day. Why? Because God created us to fellowship with Him every day since the beginning. That is the reason we are here. He loves us and He wants to have that loving interaction with Him every day. **Jeremiah 31:3** says, "The Lord has appeared of old to me, saying: "Yes, I have loved you with an everlasting love; Therefore with lovingkindness I have drawn you." In **John 15:9**, Jesus said, "As the Father loved Me, I also have loved you; abide in My love." I want to abide in that love, but I have to renew it every day. It requires a little discipline and time. So does anything else that you love. This should be first and foremost.

The Divine Order

Deuteronomy 6:5 (NKJV) "You shall love the Lord your God with all your heart, with all your soul, and with all your strength."

Matthew 22:37 "Jesus said to him, '"You shall love the Lord your God with all your heart, with all your soul, and with all your mind.' [38] This is the first and great commandment. [39] And the second is like it: 'You shall love your neighbor as yourself.' [40] On these two commandments hang all the Law and the Prophets."

Our original selfish nature kicks in at an age we cannot remember at the first hunger pang or twinge of pain and develops from there. **1 Thessalonians 5:23** says we are made up of spirit, soul, and flesh. Without the rebirth of the spirit when we believe on Jesus Christ, the natural order of things will always be what feels good (body), what makes us feel good about ourselves (soul), and maybe a little time left for some kind of spiritual activity if it benefits me and is convenient (spirit).

When we are born again (**John 3:3**), and our spirit is made alive because God's Holy Spirit has literally entered us and joined with us, the natural order has changed to the Divine order. It used to be, body, soul, and spirit. Now it becomes spirit, soul, and body. Our part now as a believer is to daily choose that order by putting the old fleshly self to death (crucifying it). **Galatians 2:20** says, "I have been crucified with Christ; it is no longer I who live, but Christ lives in me; and the life which I now live in the flesh I live by faith in the Son of God, who loved me and gave Himself for me." The problem is that we have to engage in a battle and fight for the winning side by daily denying the flesh. **Galatians 5:17** says, "For the flesh lusts against the Spirit, and the Spirit against the flesh; and these are contrary to one another, so that you do not do the things that you wish." Spiritual maturity happens as we daily agree with this verse and practice it. Grace allows us to keep starting over again when we mess up. God's Spirit gives us the power to do it.

More than ever, today, we are living in a time when we must learn to walk in the Spirit. We keep seeing the name of Jesus disgraced by carnal Christians who continue to walk after the flesh. I see Christians posting on social media things that are always about "I" and "me" and never about Jesus or things that encourage and lift up others. Some share their testimony about how they came to meet Christ and play a part on a movie that blasphemes His name or sings a song that glorifies anything but Jesus. If we want to win the world to Jesus we need to live in the Divine order. God first, others before me, and trust Him to take care of me. We need to give of ourselves to help others in any way we can, letting our actions show them Christ, then tell them about Him with our words. We need to show them that we are fulfilled and happy when we put God as the center of our life and not someone that we have to squeeze into our schedule. He said it like this: "But seek first the kingdom of God and His righteousness, and all these things shall be added to you." (**Matthew 6:33**)

The Glory of His Presence

John 17:5 (ESV) "And now, Father, glorify me in your own presence with the glory that I had with you before the world existed."

Wow! Read this verse again and ponder it. Here is Jesus, knowing He is about to be crucified along with other indescribable suffering, and He is focusing on being in the presence and full glory of the Father! That brings up so many questions, thoughts and revelations. When Jesus opened his eyes for the first time in the manger, did He just leave the glory of the presence of the Lord? Did He remember it then? If not, at what point was that a part of His memory? During His prayer times, in the wilderness, by the sea, on the mountains, like on the Mountain of Transfiguration, did He enter the glory of the presence of the Father? We know at the Transfiguration, Jesus, Moses, and Elijah were all shining with God's glory. Can you imagine, though, the time that Jesus was walking on this earth? He remembered being with the Father during the creation, during the casting out the fallen angels, during all His appearances in the Old Testament times. He knew what the unseen realm looked like, where the souls were whom He was going to preach to, where the spiritual battles took place between the angels and demons. He knew what His return and reign on the earth, the judgement, and the new Heaven and new earth would look like. He knew that the presence of the Father and His glory would get Him through the crucifixion until He said, "It is finished". But He also knew what that Psalm 22 moment would be like when the glory would be held back and He would cry, "My God, my God, why hast thou forsaken me?" That moment when He took on all our sins and became the Sacrifice; He paid for our sins. After that, Jesus entered back into the glory and the presence forever.

There are times in all of our lives when we go through sufferings and trials that we cannot endure ourselves. During those times, we need to focus on the fullness of the glory that Jesus was talking about. We need to "set our minds on things above, not things of the earth." (Colossians 3:2). Luke 24:26 says, "Ought not the Christ to have suffered these things and to enter into His glory?" Isaiah 2:10 says, "Enter into the rock, and hide in the dust, from the terror of the Lord and the glory of His majesty." How do we get into the presence of the glory of the Father? We enter into the Rock. We place ourselves in the arms of Jesus who went through the suffering for us so we could enter with Him into the glory of the Father. This helps us understand Colossians 1: 27, "To them God willed to make known what are the riches of the glory of this mystery among the Gentiles: which is Christ in you, the hope of glory ."

Here is a quick preview of this glory that Jesus was talking about: Revelation 1:12 "Then I turned to see the voice that spoke with me. And having turned I saw seven golden lampstands, [13] and in the midst of the seven lampstands One like the Son of Man, clothed with a garment down to the feet and girded about the chest with a golden band. [14] His head and hair *were* white like wool, as white as snow, and His eyes like a flame of fire; [15] His feet *were* like fine brass, as if refined in a furnace, and His voice as the sound of many waters; [16] He had in His right hand seven stars, out of His mouth went a sharp two-edged sword, and His countenance was like the sun shining in its strength." Lord, please help me enter in.

The Living Word

Hebrews 4:12 (NKJV)

"For the word of God is living and powerful, and sharper than any two-edged sword, piercing even to the division of soul and spirit, and of joints and marrow, and is a discerner of the thoughts and intents of the heart."

God's Word is alive! When the Holy Spirit lives in you, He will help you see things in it that no Bible or seminary class can teach you. When the Holy Spirit is your teacher, He can show you things directly from the written Word that pertains directly to something in your life right now. I've been reading through the Bible again, and have been seeing things that I have never noticed before coming from some of the most obscure verses from books like Numbers, Deuteronomy, and right now, Job. His Word will change you and make you more alive. It is called the "Word of Life" (**Phil. 2:16, 1 John 1**) and it literally gives you more life in your spirit, soul, and body. The devil says, "you don't have time to read it". The truth is, whatever was taking up that time is less important than reading God's Word. Eat it! Gorge on it! Don't just read "the verse of the day". That would be like taking one spoonful of food a day. Live it, know it, let it become a regular part of your conversation, thinking, and life. Let it transform you. It will change you and you will change the world.

The Mess of Manasseh

2 Chronicles 33:12-13 (ESV) "And when he was in distress, he entreated the favor of the Lord his God and humbled himself greatly before the God of his fathers. ¹³ He prayed to him, and God was moved by his entreaty and heard his plea and brought him again to Jerusalem into his kingdom. Then Manasseh knew that the Lord was God."

Manasseh's dad, Hezekiah, was probably the greatest king of Judah since David. He worshiped God, tore down all the altars to false gods, and brought God's people back to the Lord. When confronted by the Assyrians who surrounded Jerusalem with insurmountable odds, he humbled himself before God, prayed, and God defeated Sennacherib, king of Assyria. He sent him back home with his tail tucked between his legs. God send an angel to slay 185,000 troops overnight because Hezekiah humbled himself and prayed to Him.

Manasseh was a different story. As soon as his dad died, he was the typical rebellious 12 year old king. According to **2 Chronicles 33:2**, He did evil in the sight of the Lord according to the abominations of the nations of all the nations that Israel was supposed to cast out. He built altars to the fallen angels and false gods, he consulted mediums, wizards, and sorcerers, he caused his sons to pass through the fire, worshiping the god, Molech. He did everything possible to make God mad. He made the Prodigal Son look like a Boy Scout. In verse 10, it says, "And the Lord spoke to Manasseh and his people, but they would not listen." When God spoke to him, that must have been the speech with "or else" in it, because the next step was that the captains of the army of Assyria took Manasseh with hooks, bound him with bronze fetters, and carried him off to Babylon." Then, without any long story in between, he repented; just like the Prodigal Son. He humbled himself and prayed, God was moved, returned him to Jerusalem, and the greatest line here is: "Then Manasseh knew that the Lord was God." It reminds me of mom and her peach tree switch where she showed me her tough love and afterwards, "I knew that the Lord was God." I am so thankful for her faithfulness today, knowing that she loved me enough to train me up in the way of the Lord.

Today, I would like to implore my friends and loved ones who have become a mess like Manasseh. Some of you still won't admit it, but inside, you are a mess. Others acknowledge it, but you don't know what to do. Some just don't know it yet, and yet others just think you have gone too far and sunk too deep to come out of the pit. No one is more mess up than Manasseh was. No one has hit rock-bottom any further than the Prodigal Son. Jesus died on the cross to take your place. He already bore your punishment. Humble yourself and come to Him. He is ready to receive you, arms wide open.

The Peace of Jerusalem

Psalm 122:6 (NKJV)

"Pray for the peace of Jerusalem: "May they prosper who love you."

As I sit down and begin to write this (because God put it on my heart), Tauren Wells begins to speak on the Dove Awards and says the exact words I am about to write! He was saying to pray for the peace of Jerusalem, and that Jesus Christ, is the Prince of Peace! The prayer is for Jesus to reveal Himself to everyone over there, Jew, Palestinian, and everyone else. What a time for revival! As souls are quickly slipping off into eternity there, let them know Jesus. As people fear for their lives, let them call on the name of Jesus! Let the Holy Ghost pour out there as it did on the day of Pentecost! Pray this with me!

The Reason Jesus Came

1 John 3:7-9 (NKJV)

"Little children, let no one deceive you. Whoever practices righteousness is righteous, as he is righteous. [8] Whoever makes a practice of sinning is of the devil, for the devil has been sinning from the beginning. The reason the Son of God appeared was to destroy the works of the devil. [9] No one born of God makes a practice of sinning, for God's seed abides in him; and he cannot keep on sinning, because he has been born of God."

We are all familiar with **John 3:16** and about how God the Father sent His Son to come into the world that we may have eternal life if we believe. But John tells us later in **1 John**, that the reason the Son of God appeared was to destroy the works of the devil. Giving us everlasting life is destroying the works of the devil that brought about death, but in **1 John 3**, the works of the devil are also the sin in our lives while we live on this earth. When I was lost, sin had control of my life and habits. Since I have been reborn, I still sin on a daily basis, but I am no longer the slave of sin. I don't want to anymore. I care when I do and I ask God to forgive me and I repent. Like John says, I no longer practice sin. In fact, I have to practice not sinning. I can do that now, because the Savior and Redeemer lives inside of me. As I seek Jesus and draw near to Him, I can cease from sinning. When I take my eyes off of Him and put them back on myself is when I get into trouble. But here is the really good news: the Son of God appeared to destroy the works of the devil. Not to soften them or work out some sort of agreement or compromise, but to DESTROY them! Draw near to Jesus who has already destroyed the power of sin in your life on the cross. Rise with Him in His resurrection and be an overcomer where sin no longer has rule in your life!

The Set Time

Psalms 102:13 (NKJV) "You will arise and have mercy on Zion;
For the time to favor her,
Yes, the set time, has come."

There is a "set" time for everything. I was looking at a picture of the Eastern Gate in Jerusalem. This is where Ezekiel talks about the Glory of the Lord coming in the temple and a place to look for the coming of the Messiah, where many songs sing about the return of Jesus.

There is also a "set" time for everything in our lives; a time to live, a time to die, a time for specific things to happen. Especially that time when the Holy Spirit calls and we answer to receive Him into our heart.

Last night, after celebrating the football win of the Vols over the Gamecocks, my dog started barking and getting upset. I looked outside and there was a small truck at the end of my driveway with the door open. I went out and asked if I could help him. He was a small man who appeared to be somewhere between middle aged and older. He said that he was looking for this address. He showed it to me on his phone and I said, "well this is that address". I obviously wasn't who he was looking for. I told him that I was sorry I couldn't help him and started walking back to the house. Then "something" nudged me to turn around and talk some more. I started talking about how many scams were out there on the social media, etc. and something stopped me in my tracks. It hit me that this was not an accident or coincidence. I told him that. I said that it was not an accident that he had my address and that God had sent him here. I asked him if he knew Jesus and he was silent. I told him about what that meant and how to do it. I told him of my own experience. Then I asked him if he would like to ask Jesus into his life. He said, "yes". We prayed; he repented and asked God to forgive him for his sins and gave his life to Jesus Christ. This was his "set time". I don't know what he was looking for when he came, but he found something entirely different and much better than whatever is was. Pray for him that the Holy Spirit will continue to guide him to the right people and places.

Things Above

Colossians 3:1-2 (NASB) "Therefore, if you have been raised with Christ, keep seeking the things that are above, where Christ is, seated at the right hand of God. 2 Set your minds on the things that are above, not on the things that are on earth."

As I read this verse this morning, I felt a warning. Usually, when I read this, I think about not getting caught up in the world and worldly things. I think about how I need to spend more time in prayer and reading the Word. But this time, I realized that even when we are doing what we think of as "God's work", we can have our eyes "on the earth" and not above. I do a lot of volunteer work at and away from the church, visiting, teaching, counseling, helping, etc. (even writing these messages). I can get so busy doing this that I lose sight of my real purpose here on this earth. That is to fellowship with the Lord and walk with Him! That goes all the way back to the Garden with Adam and Eve. All these other activities need to be a result of this fellowship, letting His love pour through us into others. It goes back to, "I am not working for the Lord. He is working through me." I remember when my long-time friend, Pastor Lynn McWherter, said that he has to make sure that all his Bible study time is not spent preparing for the sermon the next Sunday, but that he needs that personal time for his own personal relationship with Jesus.

In **Revelation 2**, Jesus was admonishing the Church of Ephesus. When you read about their works, their faith, their diligence, their doctrinal purity, and perseverance, you would use them as a model for the perfect church even today. However, Jesus said, "but this I have against you, that you have left your first love." He, then, admonished them to repent and return to their first love. Rather than being the perfect model of a church, it became the perfect example of how a church can lose its life and light. It becomes an organization instead of an organism.

This can also happen to us as an individual. We can get caught up in our own world, routines, work, ambitions, hobbies, etc., that we look down at them rather than up into the face of God. We can even get so caught up in church work, being a missionary, feeding and helping the poor, promoting a cause, etc., that we leave our first love with Him. Jesus told us how to fix that. He said, "...remember from where you have fallen, and repent, and do the deeds you did at first...". He just wants us to keep looking at Him because He loves us. Keep looking up.

Thirsty for God

Psalm 63:1 (NKJV)

"O God, You are my God; Early will I seek You; My soul thirsts for You; My flesh longs for You In a dry and thirsty land Where there is no water."

I want to long for God like this all the time. I want to wake up in the middle of the night and spend an extra hour of prayer. I want to get up an hour earlier and do nothing but spend time with Him. Unfortunately, those times are few and far between. My spirit wants to do all these things constantly, my soul longs for these times when it's not distracted, and my flesh wants to always be lazy or self-satisfying. This is where free will comes in. I can take charge over the flesh and say, "nope". The more we do this, the more we are used to it and we, as a result, have that blessed, sacred, holy, wonderful, time with the Lord. That's where we can enter in to His presence and be re-filled, restored, and move on farther into His kingdom.

Romans 8:1

"There is therefore now no condemnation to those who are in Christ Jesus, who do not walk according to the flesh, but according to the Spirit. 2 For the law of the Spirit of life in Christ Jesus has made me free from the law of sin and death. 3 For what the law could not do in that it was weak through the flesh, God did by sending His own Son in the likeness of sinful flesh, on account of sin: He condemned sin in the flesh, 4 that the righteous requirement of the law might be fulfilled in us who do not walk according to the flesh but according to the Spirit. 5 For those who live according to the flesh set their minds on the things of the flesh, but those who live according to the Spirit, the things of the Spirit."

Hungry and thirsty? Don't wait until circumstances drive you there. Walk with Jesus daily. He is the **Bread of Life (John 6:35)** and the **Living Water (John 4:14)**.

This World Is Not My Home

Revelation 20:1-6 (NKJV) "Then I saw an angel coming down from heaven, having the key to the bottomless pit and a great chain in his hand. ² He laid hold of the dragon, that serpent of old, who is *the* Devil and Satan, and bound him for a thousand years; ³ and he cast him into the bottomless pit, and shut him up, and set a seal on him, so that he should deceive the nations no more till the thousand years were finished. But after these things he must be released for a little while. ⁴ And I saw thrones, and they sat on them, and judgment was committed to them. Then *I saw* the souls of those who had been beheaded for their witness to Jesus and for the word of God, who had not worshiped the beast or his image, and had not received *his* mark on their foreheads or on their hands. And they lived and reigned with Christ for a thousand years. ⁵ But the rest of the dead did not live again until the thousand years were finished. This *is* the first resurrection. ⁶ Blessed and holy *is* he who has part in the first resurrection. Over such the second death has no power, but they shall be priests of God and of Christ, and shall reign with Him a thousand years."

I was reading Jim Denison's *Daily Article* today and this question that he asked really stood out to me. He said, "Are your hopes and dreams more at home in heaven or on earth?" This last year, I started thinking about something a lot that I had never dwelt on much before. What will I be doing during the thousand year reign of Jesus? I know there are a lot of different teachings and beliefs that would say that it is not even "a thing", but I have had dreams and what I call "downloads" or small epiphanies on this subject (thoughts that I wouldn't have considered on my own). Just think, if we, the saints, are ruling and reigning with Christ during the Millennium, there is going to be a lot of restoration or cleaning-up to do. Will I be working with nature, trees and forests, farming, or will I be working with people, rebuilding, infrastructure, and a whole new way of doing things? The Bible says we will be kings and priests and we will be ruling and reigning with Him. I can't imagine what that will entail. It's like when we were children and we were thinking about what we were going to do when we grew up (still trying to figure that out). Whatever it is, we will be working for the King of Kings and there won't be any more political parties, campaigning, elections, mud-slinging, ignorance, or foolishness. We will have the perfect government; a totally benevolent monarchy, led by Jesus himself!

I believe, without the curse from the Garden of Eden, the weather will be what it was intended to be, the diseases will be gone, no more pain, sorrow, war, lying, cheating, hurting others, mosquito and tick bites… you get it. We may have to wait until the New Heaven and the New Earth to experience all of that. Life during the Millennium may have more gradual changes if mankind has to restore that which it destroyed. Of course, anything here mentioned that is not in the Bible is speculation, imagination, and maybe a little inspiration. Regardless, there is nothing wrong with thinking about God's Kingdom. **Colossians 3:2** says, "Set your mind on things above, not on things on the earth." **Philippians 4:8** says, "Finally, brothers, whatever is true, whatever is honorable, whatever is just, whatever is pure, whatever is lovely, whatever is commendable, if there is any excellence, if there is anything worthy of praise, think about these things." **Romans 14:17** says, "for the kingdom of God is not eating and drinking, but righteousness and peace and joy in the Holy Spirit." So, thinking about the Kingdom of God is not only thinking about Heaven, the Millennium, or the New Heaven and Earth, it is thinking about His kingdom on this earth. Righteousness, peace, joy, honor, justice, purity, good, and loveliness. When we do that, we are thinking about God's kingdom here. When we think about Heaven, we are thinking about His kingdom there. My friend, who recently went to Heaven, was in hospice and during his final hours, was sharing with us a dream he had. He was in Heaven talking to Jesus. He would tell us what Jesus said as if he was seeing it in Heaven and telling it to us on earth. The truth is, we are to do the same thing. That is, to walk in God's kingdom, and we are to deliver it here on earth. We are ambassadors of our new Kingdom. For believers in Jesus, our citizenship is no longer on this earth, so we live here, but we look forward to going home.

Philippians 3:20 "For our citizenship is in heaven, from which we also eagerly wait for a Savior, the Lord Jesus Christ."

Time to Live the Truth

---

1 John 4:1 (NKJV) "Beloved, do not believe every spirit, but test the spirits to see whether they are from God, for many false prophets have gone out into the world. ² By this you know the Spirit of God: every spirit that confesses that Jesus Christ has come in the flesh is from God, ³ and every spirit that does not confess Jesus is not from God. This is the spirit of the antichrist, which you heard was coming and now is in the world already. ⁴ Little children, you are from God and have overcome them, for he who is in you is greater than he who is in the world. ⁵ They are from the world; therefore they speak from the world, and the world listens to them. ⁶ We are from God. Whoever knows God listens to us; whoever is not from God does not listen to us. By this we know the Spirit of truth and the spirit of error."

The world is full of people who deny the Truth. They deny the Jesus is the Christ, God who came in the flesh. Those who opposed God used to use the tactic of watering down the Truth, now they openly deny Him. Now it has become the norm for those who proclaim the Truth to be the "bad guys". If you stand for Biblical family, against Biblical immorality; if you do not go along with the literal genocide of killing unborn babies, or if you do not berate God's nation of Israel, you are called out by the followers of this spirit of antichrist that is now already in the world.

I watch the protesters against Israel, who have been indoctrinated that anything against Biblical teaching is wrong and it reminds me of the pictures of the Hitler youth in the 30s and 40s. They blindly follow an ideology that was introduced by a man who, I believe, was inhabited by Satan himself. The charisma and cunning of this man went beyond human ability. His followers caved in to the fear of the sentiment of the masses of public opinion around them. They encouraged each other in it until it became the new morality. I believe that was one of the several attempts of Satan to implement the reign of the Beast mentioned in Revelation 13 Even, some of the same tactics were used mentioned Revelation and Daniel. But it was not God's timing.

Now the spirit of the world is seen again in news media, social media, movies, books, and television and it is in unity. The overall sentiment is that God's people, His Word, and God himself are wrong and "whatever I want" is right. This is the spirit of antichrist, and it is already in the world. They don't have a visible Hitler figure yet, but the ideology is there and he will come on the scene when the Church has finished its job and is no longer here.

That brings me to this final part. What I just talked about was pretty gloomy, but here's the good news. Verse 4 says, "Little children, you are from God and have overcome them, for he who is in you is greater than he who is in the world." It doesn't say, "hang in there and you might survive". It says you have already overcome them because greater is He who is in you than he who is in the world! We have already won! Now, it is imperative that we go and tell it to the world. There are still many who are seeking God and will respond if we offer Jesus to them. We need to stand for Christ, live what we believe, and walk in that victory that Jesus gave us when He overcame death. This is why we are here and alive today. We are not here to "climb the ladder of success" or "make something of ourselves" anymore. We are here to bring the Kingdom of God to the world until Jesus literally comes and fulfills it. So, let's go!

True God is Creator

Romans 9:20 (NKJV) "But indeed, O man, who are you to reply against God? Will the thing formed say to him who formed it, "Why have you made me like this?" 21 Does not the potter have power over the clay, from the same lump to make one vessel for honor and another for dishonor?"

The true God is our Creator. The false god is the one we create. The false god was created to serve us by giving false comfort, excusing our sin by saying there is no sin or it's ok to sin. The true God created everything with a design and a purpose; that purpose being to fellowship with Him, worship Him, serve Him, love Him as He loves us. He is a personal, real, living God whom we can interact with every day, all day, one-on-One.

The false god, is in church buildings all over the world. 1 John 4:3 "and every spirit that does not confess that Jesus Christ has come in the flesh is not of God. And this is the spirit of the Antichrist, which you have heard was coming, and is now already in the world." The true God, is also in the buildings, and on the street, and in the fields, or wherever the true Church is because He is inside us (**Col. 1:27**), and we are in Him (**2 Cor. 5:17**).

The non-believer cannot figure out what we believe because it cannot be grasped in the natural mind. **1 Cor. 2:14** says the natural man cannot receive the things of God because they are foolishness to him, neither can he know them because they are spiritually discerned. So, be patient, love, pray. Remember what you were like before He came in and transformed your life.

Now that He lives in me, I can start the day out saying, "I love you Papa". "Maker, what do You have in store for me today?" I open His book and He speaks to me. I walk with Him and talk with Him during the day and He speaks to me. Then I am so glad that He is not something my imagination created, but the One who created me and is daily changing me to be what He created me to be.

Two Choices

Deuteronomy 30:19 (NKJV) "I call heaven and earth as witnesses today against you, that I have set before you life and death, blessing and cursing; therefore choose life, that both you and your descendants may live; ²⁰ that you may love the Lord your God, that you may obey His voice, and that you may cling to Him, for He is your life and the length of your days; and that you may dwell in the land which the Lord swore to your fathers, to Abraham, Isaac, and Jacob, to give them."

In the Garden of Eden, Adam and Eve had two choices. The fruit was hanging there representing these choices. The choices were God's way or my way. God's way was abundant life with fruit from every other tree that was unimaginable. Never walking in fear, depression, hatred, jealously, anger, confusion, doubt. No mosquito bites, sickness, tiredness, boredom. No death.

The other choice was, do it my way. And we know the rest.

We still have those choices. We still have the option to choose life. Every day we, as believers, can choose to walk in the Spirit (life) or walk in the flesh (death). We can do something as an action of loving God and others before ourselves or we can do what's comfortable and convenient for me.

For the one who hasn't met Jesus yet, it's back to the fruit. You can pick from the Tree of Life (Jesus) by turning your back on the forbidden fruit and saying yes to Life. After that you are born again and transformed from death to life.

Now, He even helps us make those daily life/death choices by His Holy Spirit who now lives in us. So, with the Word of God showing us what to do and the Holy Spirit enabling us to do that... choose life.

Vapor

James 4:14 (NKJV) "…whereas you do not know what *will happen* tomorrow. For what *is* your life? It is even a vapor that appears for a little time and then vanishes away."

As I look outside this morning, I see a frost on the rooftop that will soon fade away with the sun shining on it and I see the fog that will soon disappear. I think of James 4:14 that says, "whereas you do not know what will happen tomorrow. For what is your life? It is even a vapor that appears for a little time and then vanishes away." I think of preaching that last Sunday at our church yesterday and couldn't believe that those twelve, plus, years had passed so quickly. Then, it hit me how the trip to Israel is right upon me, how it will begin, then it will seem like it's over almost before it starts. I can remember things as far back as when I was three years old, my six-year-old birthday party when I got a Candyland game and then moved out to the country. I remember graduation like it was just the other day and our fiftieth reunion is coming up this year. Of course, I remember when the kids were born, but now some of the grandkids are old enough to have kids, one more is graduating this year and all of them are at least old enough for school next year. I could go on and on, but you get it. My memory can flash back in an instant and come back to the "present".

When we stand before our Maker, our life will be like that. That day will be here, and we will say, "where did it go"? "It was just a vapor". Then, the only thing that will matter will be what we did in Christ. No amount of accomplishments, money, success, achievements, notability, popularity, fun, religious or secular activities, or anything else that wasn't done out of faith in Jesus Christ and His love will matter (**Matthew 25:31-46**). If our "vapor" vanishes and we have spent our life seeking satisfaction for ourselves, we will have never been satisfied and we will have missed the mark. If we have spent our lives seeking first the Kingdom of God and blessing others, we will hear the words "well done" (**Matt. 25:21**).

Vines

Luke 21:34 (ESV) "But watch yourselves lest your hearts be weighed down with dissipation and drunkenness and cares of this life, and that day come upon you suddenly like a trap.

Yesterday, I was walking through the woods with my lightweight, battery powered chainsaw with the intent of cutting the multitude of vines off of many of the trees that seemed to be being pulled down by them. I was thinking that the vines weren't actually pulling them as I imagined, and being mostly wild grape vines, they weren't sucking the life out of the trees. So why were there already a few trees that were laying on the ground? Some of the grape vine trunks were as big as a small tree. As I began to cut them near the base, water came gushing out just as if I had cut a water pipe. These vines were full of water (sap) and weighed a tremendous amount. I Googled it and asked if this was harmful to the trees. The quick answer that popped up was that between the leaves from the vines blocking out the leaves on the trees, the vines robbing nutrients from the soil, and mostly, the weight of the vines, damaged and even killed the trees.

Jesus talked about "vines" in our lives. In **Luke 21**, He said not to let our hearts be weighed down with dissipation (carousing), drunkenness, and cares (worries) of this life. The vines on the trees started out very small and not noticeable. The vines that wrap around our hearts start out as small, insignificant things. I'm reading *The Fifth Great Awakening and Future of America* by Dr.s Jim and Ryan Denison. In the chapter, "Why Pray?", it portrays a fictitious, worldwide convention called by Satan where he tells the demons to use the subtle method of making Christians non-effective. He tells them to "keep them busy with the nonessentials of life", "to overstimulate their minds" by always watching TV, listening to the radio, on the phone, etc. with no quiet time, be excessive in recreation where it drains rather than refreshes, and even in ministry like evangelism, get so busy that they run on their own strength and wear down.

These were some good examples of the vines that start out little and grow without us noticing them. Then there are the obvious vines of sin mentioned before. These also start out small and subtly. Most of them start as a distraction or diversion; the small increase in the pain medicine that was prescribed, the extra helping of food, the scheduling of too many things that take away time from the family. Getting so involved in, even Church functions, that you are missing spending time with the kids, spouses, others. Now the obvious one is being so hooked on electronic devices, that you are looking down more than you are looking up. I could continue to write a whole book on these and still leave some out.

How do I avoid or stop these "vines"? The best way is to look for them daily and literally nip them at the bud. But the ones that sneak by and become big need to be amputated. In Scriptural terms, we call this repentance. Time to go to the knees and say, "Lord, I'm sorry". Please remove this from my life and come and clean me out again. When we start off each day praying, do the inspection during the part that says "lead us not into temptation, but deliver us from evil…". Cut off the vines before they have time to grow.

Walk Close To Him

Galatians 5:16 (NKJV) "I say then: Walk in the Spirit, and you shall not fulfill the lust of the flesh."

Romans 8:1 "There is therefore now no condemnation to those who are in Christ Jesus, who do not walk according to the flesh, but according to the Spirit."

Psalms 23:4 "Yea, though I walk through the valley of the shadow of death,
I will fear no evil;
For You *are* with me;
Your rod and Your staff, they comfort me."

This morning, I was outside praying and my mind began to wander off to places, wondering how this or that was going to work out, how I was going to accomplish this, what was God going to do next, and so on. As usual, He did not give me any of those answers because He told us in **Matthew 6:34**, He said, "Therefore do not worry about tomorrow, for tomorrow will worry about its own things. Sufficient for the day is its own trouble." He also told us in the same sermon, when we pray to ask for our "daily bread" for this day (not the next). He gave enough manna in the wilderness for that one day, not the next. Why?? Listen to this:

God did not put us here to accomplish stuff; He put us here to fellowship with Him!!! He put us in the Garden to walk and fellowship with Him. He has redeemed and restored us to come back into fellowship and walk with Him. When we are tempted, we walk close to Him. When we fail, we draw back close to Him and walk with Him. When we are staring at death, in the presence of evil, when in pain, fear, confusion, doubt, despair, we walk close to Him. And to answer, what are we going to do about the situation tomorrow? We walk close to Him. He is right beside you. If you are His, He is inside of you. Just talk to Him.

"And He walks with me, and He talks with me
And He tells me I am His own
And the joy we share, as we tarry there
None other has ever known."
(From *In the Garden*, public domain).

Until My Kingdom Comes

Luke 22:15 (NKJV) "Then He said to them, "With *fervent* desire I have desired to eat this Passover with you before I suffer; [16] for I say to you, I will no longer eat of it until it is fulfilled in the kingdom of God."
[17] Then He took the cup, and gave thanks, and said, "Take this and divide *it* among yourselves; [18] for I say to you, I will not drink of the fruit of the vine until the kingdom of God comes."
[19] And He took bread, gave thanks and broke *it,* and gave *it* to them, saying, "This is My body which is given for you; do this in remembrance of Me."

2 Peter 3 says: "[10] But the day of the Lord will come as a thief in the night, in which the heavens will pass away with a great noise, and the elements will melt with fervent heat; both the earth and the works that are in it will be burned up. [11] Therefore, since all these things will be dissolved, what manner *of persons* ought you to be in holy conduct and godliness, [12] looking for and hastening the coming of the day of God, because of which the heavens will be dissolved, being on fire, and the elements will melt with fervent heat? [13] Nevertheless we, according to His promise, look for new heavens and a new earth in which righteousness dwells."

Jesus said that He would no longer eat of the Passover until it is fulfilled in the Kingdom of God. Then He said, "I will not drink of the fruit of the vine until the kingdom of God comes. The Body and the Blood in the Lord's Supper represent Jesus Himself giving His body and blood to make the ultimate sacrifice to allow us to come into the kingdom of God. When He returns, we are going to have the greatest Communion in the universe, because we are going to encounter Jesus Himself coming to us as the Groom joins with the Bride as depicted in Revelation 21. No one completely understands this, but it will be exceedingly, abundantly, beyond all that we can ask or think. That is why Jesus said that He was going to wait until He sees us again. He is as excited about reuniting with us as we should be about Him. That is why Peter, who was sitting right there by Jesus at that supper, said we should be looking for that day and literally hastening its coming. We recently went on a ten day vacation and according to my daughter, my dog, Annie, would go to a certain window and watch for us every day.

When we finally returned, she "attacked" us at the door, jumping, licking, and clinging to us. I took her out for a walk and she would take a few steps, then come running back and loving on me again because she was so glad we were back. That is the way we should be looking for Jesus to come back for us. When we take the bread and the cup; that is what we are doing. That's why my wife and I try to take it every day. We are remembering Him. We are saying, "I am watching and waiting." How does that "hasten the day"? Because when we are watching and waiting, we are doing God's will, thus letting Him work through us. We are bringing His kingdom to this earth.

Wayfaring Stranger

2 Samuel 12:4 (NKJV) "And a traveler came to the rich man, who refused to take from his own flock and from his own herd to prepare one for the wayfaring man who had come to him; but he took the poor man's lamb and prepared it for the man who had come to him."

I've read this Scripture dozens of times and never noticed this. This is in the middle of the story where King David messed up big-time by committing adultery with Bathsheba and had her husband, Uriah, put in a place where he was guaranteed to be killed in battle to cover it up. His plan almost worked, until Nathan came along. I imagine a little time went by and David thought he had gotten away with it, but God called him out in front of everyone with a prophecy and a parable. David was completely out of character with the man who had walked so closely to God for so many years. We often hear it preached where it was the time of year where Kings went to battle and David stayed home (2 Samuel 11:1), but David had a lot of other distractions going on too. He was ruling the mightiest kingdom in the world at the time. He was comfortable, successful, popular, and had all the power that went along with that. That made him vulnerable to one thing he wasn't expecting. The tempter. Nothing indicated that he was doing anything wrong until that point. He had been outwardly doing all the right things, but inwardly, he had quit drawing close to God. He probably still prayed, went to the temple, sacrificed, worshiped, and did all the things he always did, but that intimacy with God was not there. The church of Ephesus was just like that. They had all the right programs, outreaches, missions, doctrine, worship, and everything that a church should be doing, yet they failed to keep "the main thing, the main thing". They left their first love (Revelation 2:4).

Ok, here's the part that jumped out at me: when Nathan brought God's message to David, the parable told about a man who had plenty, but a *wayfaring man*, (traveling man), came by and it seems he wasn't interested in any of the rich man's sheep. He wanted the lamb that belonged to the poor man. Everything in the analogy fit David's situation except the traveling man. Who was this "wayfaring stranger"? Then it hit me. In Job 1:7, God asks Job, "From where do you come?". He answered, "From going to and fro (wayfaring) on the earth, and from walking back and forth on it." 1 Peter 5:8 says, "Be sober, be vigilant; because your adversary the devil *walks about* (wayfaring) like a roaring lion, seeking whom he may devour." This unseen wandering stranger was the devil! David was busy, caught up in doing what he thought identified him. He didn't recognize the temptation was the enemy who had found a chink in his armor.

One thing that impresses me in this reading is how David seemed wake to up when he received this splash of cold water and slap in the face from God's Word. In verse 13, " So David said to Nathan, "I have sinned against the LORD." What impressed me the most is what God said. "…And Nathan said to David, "The LORD also has put away your sin; you shall not die." David had to suffer quite a few consequences, but the prodigal son had come home. Even though David had all the distractions, temptations, and comforts that one could have at that time, today, in America, we have many more. King David didn't have AC, internet, DoorDash, TV, social media, video games, and all the other things that take our devotion away from the Lord. David's downfall wasn't that he was a bad guy. He just took his eyes off of the Lord. Twice in the Bible, he was called "a man after God's own heart" (1 Sam. 13:14, Acts 13:22).

The way this applies to us is, we are no better than David. We are even more distracted than he was. The same "wayfaring stranger" is still wandering around seeking whom he may devour. The truth is, we will be tempted, we will fail, but we have one advantage. As believers in Jesus Christ, He lives inside of us. He redeems our sins and failures. He turns plan X,Y,and Z back into plan A. Then He makes us as if we never sinned. He makes us what He originally intended us to be. That is what Colossians 1:27 means when it says "To them God willed to make known what are the riches of the glory of this mystery among the Gentiles: which is **Christ in you, the hope of glory."**

We Are In That Time

Over the last 52 years I've known Jesus, I have been accused of being an "end-times" preacher. If you've listened to the majority of my sermons, I am preaching on walking with Jesus, being a disciple, salvation, what God can do in your life, and on and on, but the majority of them have not been focused on a Second-Coming sermon. However, I do refer to the times that we live in, how the events of the world line up with Bible prophecy, the rapture, and Jesus coming back in almost every sermon. Why? Am I obsessed with it? No. That's just the times that we are living in. No hype, no sensationalism, just fact. The fact is, if there were absolutely no Bible prophecies about the end times, our world is in a state where it could not continue to survive. But the truth is, every Bible prophecy that needs to be fulfilled before the rapture of the Church has been fulfilled. There are a couple, like the rebuilding of the temple, that need to happen during the Great Tribulation, but everything else is ready. People will tell you that all this has happened before, but never before in history have we lived in a time when Israel has been restored as a nation in one day until May 14, 1948, fulfilling this prophecy: **Isaiah 66:8 (NKJV)** "Who has heard such a thing? Who has seen such things? Shall the earth be made to give birth **in one day**? *Or* shall a nation be born at once? For as soon as Zion was in labor, She gave birth to her children."

In 1967, I remember watching the news and seeing how the Israelis defeated the Arab countries surrounding them in six days, being outnumbered 90 to 1. (They got to rest on the 7th day). We are seeing nations align with each other predicted in **Ezekiel 38**. We see the exact technology in existence now needed to produce the mark of the Beast in Revelation 13. We see the wars, rumors of wars, famines, pestilence, etc., mentioned in **Matthew 24, Luke 22, and Mark 13**, happening now.

The odds of all these scriptures being fulfilled (not to mention exact dates and events in Daniel 11 and 12) not being a coincidence are greater than that of winning the Powerball multiple times in the same day. The chances of all the prophecies in the Bible, (spread out over 2500 years, written by different people, that have been fulfilled), being a "coincidence" are around 10^{2000} to one against it. That is 1 with 2000 zeroes behind it. If something has odds against it of 10^{50}, it is written off as scientifically "impossible". Scientifically and mathematically, it is impossible, forty times over, for these Biblical prophecies not to be true. That being established, let's look at this one last prophecy said by Jesus Himself: Matthew 24: [33] So you also, when you see all these things, know that it is near—at the doors! [34] Assuredly, I say to you, ***this generation will by no means pass away till all these things take place.*** Are you ready?

We Are Protected

1 John 5:18-21 (ESV) "We know that everyone who has been born of God does not keep on sinning, but he who was born of God protects him, and the evil one does not touch him.[19] We know that we are from God, and the whole world lies in the power of the evil one.[20] And we know that the Son of God has come and has given us understanding, so that we may know him who is true; and we are in him who is true, in his Son Jesus Christ. He is the true God and eternal life. [21] Little children, keep yourselves from idols".

Verse 18, and similar verses in 1 John used to confuse me and even worry me. I would think, I've been born of God, yet I would still not make it through a day without sinning. Then the obvious question would come, "Am I really born of God?" The answer lies within the same verse. It says "…but he who was born of God protects him and the evil one does not touch him." Jesus, the Son of God erased our sin and is at the right hand of the Father, advocating for us (**1 John 2:1-2**). When the accuser, the devil (**Rev. 12:10**) points out our sins to the Father, Jesus overrides that accusation, showing that He paid for our sins already. And He does it eternally (**Romans 8:26, Hebrews 7:25**), because when Jesus paid for our sins, He did it once and for all on the cross (**Hebrews 7:27, 9:12, 10:10**).

So, verse 19 says the whole world lies in the power of the evil one, but we are not of this world anymore. Jesus protects us because we are in Him if we believe on Him, so we no longer live under the dominion of Satan. Jesus, the true God and eternal life also literally lives in us. There is no other god who does that. That is why the last verse says, "Little children, keep yourselves from idols." There is no other god who can sit at the right hand of the Father, who has overcome the devil and death, who has paid for our sins by taking our place, who protects us and keeps us. No one but Jesus.

Well Done

Matthew 25:21 (NKJV)
"His lord said to him, 'Well done, good and faithful servant; you were faithful over a few things, I will make you ruler over many things. Enter into the joy of your lord.'"

This morning, I was thinking about how the Lord could say "well done" to someone like me who constantly finds ways to mess up. In this verse, He says, "...you were faithful over a few things..." Narrow it down even more; "faithful". What does that mean? You believe. You don't quit believing, even when you mess up. Ask King David. Boy, he messed up, big time, more than once. Yet, **1 Sam.13:14** and **Acts 13:22** say he was a man after God's own heart. Why? Because he never quit believing. He would repent and turn away from the sin. He suffered some consequences, but he never quit believing and loving God. Jesus said, "I will never leave you, nor forsake you." (**Hebrews 13:5**). **Romans 4** says that Abraham's faith was counted as righteousness to him. Adam, Eve, and all the rest of humanity messed up because of not believing God and His Word. Jesus is telling us to believe, stay connected, continue to love Him and follow Him. He will take care of the rest. He will continue to correct, adjust, tweak, and lead us in the right direction. Then when we are though, He will say, "Well done!"

When I Fall, I Will Arise

Micah 7:7-8 (NKJV)

"⁷ Therefore I will look to the Lord;
I will wait for the God of my salvation;
My God will hear me.
⁸ Do not rejoice over me, my enemy;
When I fall, I will arise;
When I sit in darkness,
The Lord *will be* a light to me."

This is such good news for a believer! It is my story! In our new life, we have a Redeemer. When we fall, because of Jesus, we will arise. When we mess up, when we wander into the dark, He will be our light and put us back on track. The first verse, "Therefore I will look to the Lord" is our answer. In everything; every day; then we wait for the God of our salvation (He will save us from the present troubles-(**Psalm 46:1**). And the end of verse 7 says, "MY GOD WILL HEAR ME". It's in writing. Guaranteed.

When You Pray

Luke 11:1 (NKJV) "Now it came to pass, as He was praying in a certain place, when He ceased, that one of His disciples said to Him, "Lord, teach us to pray, as John also taught his disciples." ² So He said to them, "When you pray, say:..."

Notice Jesus didn't say, "if you pray", but "when you pray". The prayer right after this (also in **Matthew 6:8-13**) was never intended to be a mantra to repeat over and over. It was a model or outline showing us how to pray. Prayer is simply talking to God, not repeating words that are coming from memory and not our heart. For the next few days, I want to look at how each part of the Lord's prayer or model prayer is an outline showing us how to enter into His presence and talk to Him about our greatest needs or smallest thoughts. The world mocks us, saying "we don't need your thoughts and prayers". I agree with them on one part. The world doesn't need our thoughts; we can keep them to ourselves. It needs our prayers though. **James 5:16** says that the effective, fervent prayer of a righteous person avails much. **Revelation 5:8** says our prayers are stored up as incense before the Lord.

Who Is Your King?

Judges 21:25 (NKJV) "In those days there was no king in Israel; everyone did what was right in his own eyes".

This is one of the saddest verses in the Bible. There are many victories in the book of Judges, but it has a sad ending. All throughout the book, God's people are doing their own thing, worshiping idols, breaking all the commandments, trying to worship God in their own way. In one place, some of the tribe of Benjamin commit the same abominations as the people of Sodom and Gomorra. They even fight among themselves and kill off almost the entire tribe of Benjamin.

Does that sound familiar? I'm not talking about the world today, I'm talking about the church. In the days of the Judges, they had the law to govern and judge the people. The people decided to ignore it and do their own thing. Today, many of the people who call themselves the church are wandering aimlessly trying to follow God their own way. What they are doing doesn't satisfy, so they try to add other things, beliefs, and activities to their Christianity that don't align with God's Word. They follow their "gut" and do what feels right or seems right in their own eyes. It just becomes another religion, not the living relationship that Jesus intended it to be.

The true Church has the Bible and the Holy Spirit there to lead us. We have the personal relationship with Jesus that keeps us connected to Him every day. We are constantly growing and changing and becoming more like God created us to be. We have fellowship with other believers to strengthen ourselves and each other. We don't have to do what is "right in our own eyes" when we really don't have a clue, because we have a King. There cannot be two Kings in one realm. You have to step down off your throne to allow Jesus to come and take His rightful place. Is Jesus King of your life?

Why By Faith?

Hebrews 11:6 (NKJV) "And without faith it is impossible to please him, for whoever would draw near to God must believe that he exists and that he rewards those who seek him."

Romans 14:23b "For whatever does not proceed from faith is sin."

Hebrews 11:24-25 "By faith Moses, when he was grown up, refused to be called the son of Pharaoh's daughter, 25 choosing rather to be mistreated with the people of God than to enjoy the fleeting pleasures of sin."

Why is it so important to do things by faith? Why does it please God? Why is it even sin, not to do it by faith? Because faith connects us to God. Faith releases the kingdom of God to function through us. Anything that we do on this earth that will be remembered and rewarded in God's kingdom will be those things that were actually done through us by the Holy Spirit. Not by us for the Lord, but through us; us in conjunction with Him. Why? Because He created us to be one with Him, to fellowship with Him and when we are reborn, Jesus dwells inside of us.

Moses could have chosen to use his position in Pharaoh's palace to smoothly transition things when he grew in power to release the Hebrew children. That would have made a lot of sense; even common sense. It was a good political move. But God had other plans. The Israelites were delivered from more than slavery to the Egyptians. They were delivered from slavery to sin, idols, demons, and a way of thinking. You can only be delivered from those things supernaturally. You can only be supernaturally delivered from something by getting help from God, and you can only get help from God by faith.

Today, you may or may not know what God has called you to do or be. God called Moses to deliver 2 ½ million people from spiritual death. But He didn't do it Moses' way. God has a plan for you, but don't try to figure out how it's going to happen. Don't try to make it happen, because it will be wrong if it's your idea. Just say, "yes Lord" and then stop and listen. If you don't hear anything, just keep drawing near to God, growing in His Word, fellowshipping with Jesus. Moses herded sheep and grew in the Lord. Seek Him and His kingdom every day, not looking at what He has called you to do, but just looking at Him. He will take care of the rest.

"Woke"

This term, "woke" has been used a lot in the last couple of years. For those who claim to be "woke", they mean "enlightened". Once, I picked up on a conversation between two guys who were both in some form of ministry. They believed that they had received an epiphany or enlightenment that had brought them to a new place in their walk with God. They had their own kind of "awakening" where they believed that they had discovered a new depth in God. Half of what they believed was right. They believed that God loved everyone no matter what. The other half was wrong. They believed that we could have that relationship with God and stay the same. In other words, you could have that relationship with God with no repentance. That's saying, we accept His love for us, but we don't love Him back. That's not a relationship. That is deception from Satan who doesn't care if we go half way as long as we don't come into a full covenantal relationship with Him, giving our lives to Him. You see, Satan told the same half-truths at the tree in the Garden of Eden. He told them to doubt God and disobey Him by eating the fruit. If they ate it, they would be enlightened or "woke", thus being "equal with God". Ha! That's what has the world in the mess that it's in right now.

Thankfully, Jesus provided a way out of that situation. He loved us so much, the Father loves us so much, that Jesus took our sin away by becoming that sin for us. He who never sinned became sin and took the blame and the punishment on the cross. (That is why it is so heinous and ridiculous to say it's ok to continue in our sinful lifestyle. That would be trying to negate what Jesus did on the cross.) So after Jesus gave up His life on the cross, on Sunday morning, He AWOKE! When we believe and receive that we awake with Him! That is being truly WOKE! **Romans 13:11 (ESV)** says, "Besides this you know the time, that the hour has come for you to wake from sleep. For salvation is nearer to us now than when we first believed."

Jesus had an even stronger term than "woke" for knowing Him. In **John 3:3**, He called it being "born again". The experience of being reborn is what brings us back into that love relationship with God that we left in the Garden. Once you fall in love with Jesus, you want to keep growing in that love. Yes, we mess up, but His love for us keeps forgiving and drawing us closer to Him (that's called grace). We grow in that love and quit loving the things that are not aligned with Him and the way He created us. If we really know Him, we do not want to sin. The closer we get to Him, the less we want to sin. Verse two says if we are "in Christ", we are new creations. Old things are passed away and all things have become new. Let's rejoice that on Resurrection morning, Jesus AWOKE and we can now be awoken with Him forever!

Work In Me

Colossians 1:29 (NKJV)
"To this *end* I also labor, striving according to His working which works in me mightily."

This morning, I was praying, thinking about God working through me, and I heard the still, small, voice saying, "I want to work *in* you". Working through me is a product of working in me. God can accomplish all sorts of things through us, but more importantly, He wants to walk with us; in us! That's what He created us for in the garden. Walking with Him now will restore us to that place, but even more important than that, we are communing together. That's how much He loves us.

Worshiping In One Accord

Acts 4:24 (NKJV)
"And when they heard that, they lifted up their voice to God with one accord, and said, Lord, thou art God, which hast made heaven, and earth, and the sea, and all that in them....
³¹ And when they had prayed, the place was shaken where they were assembled together; and they were all filled with the Holy Ghost, and they spoke the word of God with boldness.

We went to a worship gathering at the arena in Nashville over the weekend and God showed me some wonderful things. I have been in a many worship gatherings over the last 53 years, but I saw something in this one that was very significant with the time that we are living in. I am estimating that there were ten to twelve thousand people in there and during most of the singing, almost everyone was singing, worshipping, and praying with all their might. Everyone was worshipping with all their hearts and most were not holding back. In other words, we were of one accord. The worship team had no celebrities and had a wide variety of individuals. They were just worshipping with all their hearts. The worship was acknowledging God for who He is and what He has done and what He is doing now just like in Acts 4. As I was looking up, I could almost see the angels worshipping with us beyond the "veil". The mighty power of God was there. I do not believe it was because of the group, the venue, the preacher, or anything else like that. I believe that the Holy Spirit is moving on His people all over the world to come together and proclaim God's Word, power, majesty, love, because it is time. I literally felt strongholds being toppled like Jericho while this was going on. I am expecting miracles like those in the book of Acts, from souls being saved, to people being set free, to the ground shaking.

Going home and trying to imitate or emulate a certain style of worship is not going to make it happen. Christians have been doing that for generations and it just doesn't work. It will happen when it is God's timing and when we are looking up every day expecting Him (**2 Peter 3:12**). However, I believe if you are "looking up" now, walking in the Spirit, you will see and know that time is right on top of us. There will be great revival right before He comes (**Acts 2, Joel 2**). A friend of mine was in Nashville the same night with a group of people street preaching. She told me that there were a few hecklers, but several people came up and engaged and were interested in the Gospel. She thought it was miraculous how smoothly it went. I told her about the powerful prayer and worship going on right down the street. We both agreed that God had them planned together. I believe that we are in the time of the last-days Harvest. There will be much warfare just like during the time of John the Baptist and Jesus (**Matt. 11:12**). The battle will be won like in the days of Moses and Joshua when we send out Judah (the worshipers) first. Many will be saved, healed, delivered from bondage. There will be many going to Heaven who wouldn't have been because we are engaged in the battle. Worship, pray, witness! It is time.

Write It Down

Ephesians 1:16 (NKJV) "(I) do not cease to give thanks for you, making mention of you in my prayers: 17 that the God of our Lord Jesus Christ, the Father of glory, may give to you the spirit of wisdom and revelation in the knowledge of Him..."

My son called me around 6:30 this morning while driving to work to share some things that God had shown him while reading the Word. It was really profound and I hope he shares it with others. The reason he called me was, not only to share it with me, but so he wouldn't forget it. After you share something with someone else, you usually don't.

Recently, the Lord had impressed upon me to have a pad and pen by my bed so if I had a dream or thought in the middle of the night (**Acts 2**, "Old men will dream dreams..."), I would write it down so I would not forget it. Sure enough, the first test came. It was something so plain and easy to remember that I thought, "there's no way I'll forget this" so I didn't write it down. A few hours later, I woke up and it had completely left me. I learned my lesson.

Paul prayed for us that God would give us the Spirit of wisdom and revelation. I like to take that prayer and apply it to myself regularly. If we agree with that prayer and believe it, it will happen on a regular basis. We often don't realize it, but He is ready to reveal things to us every day. I believe I'm praying that when I say "give us this daily bread". It usually jumps out at me while reading or meditating on God's word. Try it out. Get your pen and pad ready.

You Be the New You

---

2 Corinthians 5:17 (NKJV) "Therefore, if anyone *is* in Christ, *he is* a new creation; old things have passed away; behold, all things have become new. ¹⁸ Now all things *are* of God, who has reconciled us to Himself through Jesus Christ, and has given us the ministry of reconciliation, ¹⁹ that is, that God was in Christ reconciling the world to Himself, not imputing their trespasses to them, and has committed to us the word of reconciliation.²⁰ Now then, we are ambassadors for Christ, as though God were pleading through us: we implore *you* on Christ's behalf, be reconciled to God. ²¹ For He made Him who knew no sin *to be* sin for us, that we might become the righteousness of God in Him."

I don't know how many times I have quoted 2 Cor. 5:17 in a regular conversation, Bible study, or sermon, but each time, the emphasis was on being the new creation, the new person that Jesus makes you when you are born again. But, it is amazing what happens when you read the other verses that go with it. God didn't make us into that new creature just to let us sit there and look pretty and take up space. He didn't even do it to make us start looking more like the original Adam or Eve. That's just an occurrence that takes place as we grow closer to Jesus. In fact, the simple reason He did it is because He loves us and wants us back in fellowship with Him. The old self couldn't do that because it was full of darkness and going away from Him. But the question doesn't need to be "why?'. It needs to be, "what do I do with this?" He could have transformed us and beamed us directly up to Heaven, but that's not the way it works. Once we are reconciled to Christ, we become reconcilers ourselves. We are ambassadors from the Kingdom of God to introduce the Kingdom to the world. We tell them how God will forgive them, delivering them from the curse and bondage of sin. We simply tell them what God did for us, then the Holy Spirit will give us the rest of what we need to say. Yes, we do it through actions also because we love them, but we always need to find that time to transform the actions to words and the words to actions. The world says, "you be you". God says, "you be the new you with Me in you".

Your Body Needs You

1 Corinthians 12:12 (NKJV) "For just as the body is one and has many members, and all the members of the body, though many, are one body, so it is with Christ."

How would you like to have to function every day without one of your body parts or one of those parts not functioning? Many people do and it makes life a lot more difficult for them. Some have to make minor adjustments like glasses or a hearing aid and others have to have life-altering changes that make life barely manageable. The Church (capital C) is the Body of Christ. If you are a believer, you are part of it. If you are not gathered with them, you are a missing part. If you go to church and are not asking, "God, how can you use me today?", you are not functioning. Some Christians are still debating with themselves whether or not they need to go to church. They have missed the whole point. The church needs them. When we become a follower of Christ, we become a part of Him. We are needed. Neither He, nor the Church, are there to serve us; we are here to serve them. How? When my foot goes to sleep, I can patiently wait for it to come around and when it does "wake up", I can get around a lot better without hobbling. We need to wake up; attach ourselves to Him by fellowshipping with Him daily, and attach ourselves to each other by being together, reaching out, talking to each other, helping each other, loving one another. And to answer the other question, "do I need the Church?" Imagine a foot standing there on the floor without a body. See you at Church!

The Same Body

---

1 Corinthians 10:15 (NKJV) I speak as to wise men; judge for yourselves what I say. [16] The cup of blessing which we bless, is it not the communion of the blood of Christ? The bread which we break, is it not the communion of the body of Christ? [17] For we, though many, are one bread and one body; for we all partake of that one bread.

In **1 Corinthians 12**, more than once, Paul says that we are the Body of Christ. In verses 12-14, is says, "For as the body is one and has many members, but all the members of that one body, being many, are one body, so also is Christ. [13] For by one Spirit we were all baptized into one body—whether Jews or Greeks, whether slaves or free—and have all been made to drink into one Spirit. [14] For in fact the body is not one member but many.

When we take the Lord's Supper together, whether we each take a small piece of bread and dip it into a common cup, or whether we take it and drink from the cups, know that the cup represents the blood of Jesus Christ that cleanses us from all sin (1 John 1:7 But if we walk in the light as He is in the light, we have fellowship with one another, and the blood of Jesus Christ His Son cleanses us from all sin). That blood washes away the sin and qualifies us to be the body of Christ or the Church. That is the "glue" or bond that holds us all together and puts us all on level ground before the Lord.

Now, imagine each small portion of bread being you. Each one is a little different from the other, some are a lot different. Each of us has a different testimony, different gifts, a different personality, but we are all necessary parts of the Body of Christ. The blood of Jesus has flowed and been absorbed into each piece and bonds us into that Body that Jesus was talking about.

When you take the bread and the cup, the Body and the Blood, look at the person beside you, in front of you, behind you, on the other side of the church, and let yourself be one with each of them as you are with Christ. Ask God to renew you and to strengthen your relationship with Him and each other. When that happens, there is no limit to what God will do in you, in them, and in the Church.

Printed in the United States
by Baker & Taylor Publisher Services